DISCARDED BY
PIERCE COLLEGE LIBRARY

D0400264

CONSPIRACY OF SILENCE
THE TRAUMA OF INCEST

◆◆◆◆◆◆◆◆◆◆◆◆◆◆◆◆◆◆◆

by Sandra Butler

VOLCANO
· PRESS ·

Copyright ©1978, 1985 by Sandra Butler. All rights reserved.

Printed in the United States of America

Library of Congress Cataloging in Publication Data

Butler, Sandra, 1938-
   Conspiracy of silence.

   Bibliography p.
   1. Incest. 2. Sex crimes—United States. I. Title.
HQ72.U53B87   301.41'58   78-1975
ISBN 0-912078-73-1

Volcano Press (formerly New Glide Publications) participates in the Cataloging in Publication Program of the Library of Congress. However, in our opinion, the data provided us for this book by CIP does not adequately nor accurately reflect its scope and content. Therefore, we are offering our librarian/users the choice between LC's treatment and an Alternative CIP prepared by Sanford Berman, Head Cataloger at Hennepin County Library, Edina, Minnesota.

Alternative Cataloging in Publication Data

Butler, Sandra, 1938-
   Conspiracy of silence: the trauma of incest.
Volcano Press, ©1978, 1985

   PARTIAL CONTENTS: The children.-The aggressors.-The mothers.-The family.-History of a survivor.

   1. Incestuous assault. 2. Incest victim services.
I. Volcano Press. II. Title. III. Title:
The trauma of incest.

362.71

Text design and composition: Zoe Brown

Jacket design: Anita Walker Scott

Appendix research: Frances Haselsteiner

Acknowledgement is made for permission to reprint from "The Transformation of Silence into Language and Action," in *Sister Outsider*. ©1984 by Audre Lorde. Crossing Press, Trumansburg, New York. Reprinted with permission of the Charlotte Sheedy Agency.

Order books directly from:

Volcano Press, Inc., P.O. Box 270, Volcano, California 95689
Telephone: 209-296-3445   Fax: 209-296-4515

Please enclose $12.95 for each copy ordered. For postage and handling, add $4.50 for the first book and $1.00 for each additional book. California residents please add appropriate sales tax.

CONTENTS

♦ ♦ ♦ ♦ ♦ ♦ ♦

To Janice, whose search for purity and integrity in her life has been a source of pride and an example for me.

To Alison, from whom I have learned the deepest and most valued lessons of motherhood and sisterhood.

FOREWORD

◆ ◆ ◆ ◆ ◆ ◆ ◆

It is seven years since Sandra Butler first defined the conspiracy of silence surrounding incest, and helped to break that silence. Looking back, it is hard to imagine that so much has changed in such a comparatively short time. Sexual abuse of children has become a focus of attention in the national media, and a subject for scholarly investigation, professional intervention, and legal reform. We now know that one girl in four is sexually abused before puberty, one in three by the age of eighteen. We have learned this, not because we doctors and social workers and reporters and police and prosecutors and lawyers and judges were interested (indeed, we were not—we were an active part of the conspiracy) but because women like Sandra Butler spoke out, and gave courage to victims to speak in their own voices.

For people who have been abused and traumatized, silence is the greatest barrier to recovery. The breaking of secrecy is the beginning of healing. Through sharing stories, the social bonds destroyed by incest are mended, and the traumatic experience is given new meaning in the retelling; it becomes a gift to others. Sandra Butler was able to do what she did because she knew how to listen respectfully, to bear witness, to make it safe for victims to break their silence, and to make it possible for victims to reach each other. It is my hope that this book finds its way into the hands of the many—still too many—professionals who would prefer to deny the problem, and the many, too many women and children, who are still keeping their secrets.

Judith L. Herman, M.D.
March 1985

PREFACE

◆◆◆◆◆◆◆

In the following pages I explore the dynamics of, and society's response to, incestuous assault. I began my research as a writer interested in reporting her findings to a general readership. Thousands of hours of interviews with hundreds of men and women, as well as research into the few currently existing counseling programs across the United States, went into the preparation of this book. As I progressed in my work and became aware of the lack of dialogue and minimal services provided to members of incest families, I found it difficult to maintain my detachment as an observer and interviewer. As a result of recognizing the dimensions of the problem and the limited and limiting approaches to it, I recently have become directly involved in a professional capacity.

Whenever possible, I have not intruded upon the voices of the men and women who shared with me some of the most painful experiences of their lives. I believe that by reporting their feelings and experiences simply and honestly I can provide some of the understanding needed for change— a change in our attitudes and misconceptions and in the limited alternatives most communities presently offer to incest victims and their families.

These pages reflect some of my anger and frustration at what I found in my research, as well as the feelings of the people who trusted me enough to reveal their experiences and without whom this book could not have been written. I hope that those whose words appear here will feel their trust has not been misplaced, and to them I extend my deepest gratitude.

There are others whose support and encouragement were vital to the completion of this book: Jeanne Adleman Mahoney, who consistently asked the critical questions that helped me develop much of my analysis and perspective; Ruth Gottstein, who offered the idea whose time was overdue; David Charlsen, whose careful reading and suggestions helped me clarify and distill much of my work; Linda Gunnarson, skilled editor and enthusiastic supporter in my bleakest hours; Joslyn Rhodes, who taught me the true meaning of the word "family"; Carole Klein, who knew long before I did that I would write and who helped me to begin; Seamon and Sadye Steen, my beloved parents, whose confidence in me and my work has been my foundation; Marinell Eva, a wise and beloved friend and Barbara Rosenblum, whose intellectual clarity challenges, and whose support nourishes.

Each of us is here now because in one way or another we share a commitment to language and to the power of language, and to the reclaiming of that language which has been made to work against us. In the transformation of silence into language and action, it is vitally necessary for each one of us to establish or examine her function in that transformation and to recognize her role as vital within that transformation.

For those of us who write, it is necessary to scrutinize not only the truth of what we speak, but the truth of that language by which we speak it. For others, it is to share and spread also those words that are meaningful to us. But primarily for us all, it is necessary to teach by living and speaking those truths which we believe and know beyond understanding. Because in this way alone we can survive, by taking part in a process of life that is creative and continuing, that is growth.

—Audre Lorde
Sister Outsider

THE SCOPE OF
THE PROBLEM
◆◆◆◆◆◆◆◆◆◆

When the idea of writing a book about incest was suggested
to me, I responded with immediate enthusiasm. It was a
subject I had never heard openly discussed, one that was
shrouded in secrecy and about which uncomfortable jokes
were made. Because incestuous behavior was outside the
realm of my own life experience, I assumed at that time
that it also was foreign to the people I knew. My research
proved otherwise.

As I began my work, the simple statement that I was preparing a book about incest elicited an overwhelming response from people needing and wanting to share their
early childhood experiences with me. The first person I
interviewed was a young woman who worked within a
child-protection services agency. As we talked, I was surprised at the large number of cases each worker was required to handle and asked the woman about the kinds of
abuse that were reported. Although most of the woman's
cases involved physical and emotional abuse within families, she admitted that sexual abuse of children within the
home was vastly underreported and unacknowledged by

social workers. That evening, I received a call at home from a woman who did not identify herself. She explained that she worked in the agency I had visited that day and had overheard my conversation with her superior. She called to see if I would be interested in hearing about her incest experiences. I assured her that I was, and we arranged to meet the following day.

At our meeting, the woman spoke without interruption for more than an hour about her four-year sexual relationship with her father. She did not spare me any of the graphic sexual or emotional details of her adolescence and thanked me for taking the time to listen to her. "I blamed myself for such a long time for letting it go on; it's a relief to talk about it without having somebody look at you as though you're some kind of freak. It's such a comfort to know that someone will try to understand," she said as we parted. But I did not understand. Not really. For I had approached this subject with many misconceptions based on a lack of knowledge and understanding of the dynamics of incestuous behavior.

The word "incest" generates a wide variety of responses in people, nearly always negative. In the dictionary incest is defined as sexual intercourse between closely related persons where marriage is legally forbidden. This can and does include consensual relationships between adults, most often brothers and sisters, and consensual relationships among children within a family who are engaging in sexual play and experimentation. The significant distinction in the majority of families I interviewed was that the nature of the incest was non-consensual—it was, in reality, incestuous assault—and I concentrated my efforts on exploring this aspect of incestuous behavior.

In this book I have used the phrase "incestuous assault" to refer to any manual, oral or genital sexual contact or other explicit sexual behavior that an adult family member imposes on a child, who is unable to alter or understand the adult's behavior because of his or her powerlessness in the family and early stage of psychological development. This type of incest is non-consensual because the child has not yet developed an understanding of sexuality that allows him or her to make a free and fully conscious response to the adult's behavior.

I have not limited my definition of incestuous assault to sexual intercourse but have expanded it to include any sexual activity or experience imposed on a child which results in emotional, physical or sexual trauma. The forms of incestuous assault are diverse; the acts are not always genital and the experience not always a physical one. The father who stations himself outside the window of his daughter's bedroom to watch her dress and undress is raping his child's mind as surely as the father who violently and forcibly rapes his child's body.

Whatever form the assault takes, the scarring of the child can be deep and lasting. Unlike physical abuse, the damage cannot always be seen, but the scars are there nonetheless. The most devastating result of the imposition of adult sexuality upon a child unable to determine the appropriateness of his or her response is the irretrievable loss of the child's inviolability and trust in the adults in his or her life.

In addition to expanding the definition of incestuous assault to include the full range of damaging sexual attitudes and behaviors imposed on children by adults, I have at the same time specifically focused on the most common patterns of such assault. This decision was not made arbitrarily. In the vast majority of reported incestuous assault cases the offender is an adult male and the child victim a female. In one study of incestuous abuse cases, 97 percent of the offenders were adult males and 87 percent of the child victims were females.[1] A study based on court cases involving incest offenses revealed that 90 percent of the cases concerned fathers and daughters, stepfathers and stepdaughters, and grandfathers and granddaughters. Of the remaining 10 percent, half were sexual relationships between fathers and sons.[2]

In attempting to emphasize the personal dynamics involved in adult male and female child assault, I have found it imperative to examine the larger issue of male-dominated family systems in the context of a male-defined society and its assumptions about sex roles and expectations. Although incestuous assault happens within a family context, the family has incorporated the values and standards of our traditional patriarchy. Therefore, as important as it is to understand the personal psychodynamics of the male sexual aggressor, it is equally important to understand male sexual aggression as an outgrowth of the patriarchal nature of male/female relationships in every aspect of our lives.

When I first began my research, I had to dispel my own set of stereotypes about families in which incestuous assault takes place. I had expected to find violent, alcoholic men—men who live in families with too little money and too many children; men who are abusive and uncaring and unfeeling; men who give vent to their distorted sexual feelings at the expense of their children, who have become dehumanized into receptacles for the outpourings of their parents' rage and frustration. I never expected to find a sexually abusive father living on my street or attending my house of worship. I was not prepared to find victims of incestuous assault among my circle of friends nor did I anticipate their eagerness to share their experiences with me.

I felt sure that I would find incestuous assault occurring primarily in ingrown mountain communities and in fragmented inner-city families, but I was wrong. What I found was a cross-section of American families who are suffering from the traumas of incestuous assault—families from all socio-economic classes, families like those I had known all my life, families that subscribe to the work ethic and whose members are upstanding pillars of their communities, civic leaders and church members. My year of research was personally exhausting as I continually found myself confronted with challenges to many of the assumptions I had made about the nature of incestuous assault.

I was depressed and angered to find such a small number of agencies offering skilled and sensitive help to families dealing with incestuous abuse problems—families these agencies have been mandated to serve and children they have been mandated to protect. Frequently the professionals in such agencies had little to say about the problem. But the silence of the professional community was countered by the number of incest victims who sought me out to share their concerns and anxieties about early, often unresolved sexual assaults upon them by members of their families.

As I traveled across the country, I found that I simply needed to send a letter explaining the nature of my research to a women's center, community organization or feminist therapy group in order to find women who were willing to talk with me. Some victims preferred to remain anonymous but spoke to me at great length on the telephone; others were grateful for the opportunity to say things aloud they had never talked about before; still others met with me to assure themselves that incestuous assault had happened in other homes and to other children. In some cases I learned more about a woman victim in just a few hours than her husband knew. The fear of outside judgment had caused many victims to hide their painful experiences from their loved ones so that their feelings remained festering inside them.

Some of the victims whose words appear on these pages have been involved in drug or alcohol abuse counseling programs, and others have been or presently are working as prostitutes; but nearly half of the 130 women interviewed are or were married and are raising their own families. Many of the victims are streetwise, and others are college-educated. But, although they expressed themselves in a variety of ways, their lives of pain and betrayal sounded very much the same. These victims were able to express grief, shame and sometimes rage once they knew that there were others like themselves—thousands and thousands of others. Although the specific details varied from person to person, the isolation victims felt in having kept the wound hidden and themselves silent remained the same. The victims thought that what had happened to them had never happened to anyone else and felt alone in their loss of faith in the persons who had assaulted them and in their rage at a world in which such assault could be permitted to occur.

The willingness of incest victims to talk with me was surprising since I had expected precisely the reverse. I had imagined that the agencies designed to serve victims and their families, doctors who had direct contact with abused children and therapists who were counseling families that were locked into abusive communication patterns would be responsive to sharing their experiences and techniques for providing successful intervention to incest families. This was seldom the case. It was in the professional community that I found the silence I had anticipated finding among those who had been victimized. Again and again as I sought out men and women with the training and experience that should have equipped them with the foundation upon which to develop alternatives in treatment and counseling, I heard the same phrase: "We don't see much of that here."

After spending many months interviewing victims, aggressors and other family members, I began to understand the reason for the incest family's "secret"—the fear of exposing the family to the outraged scrutiny of the community— but I could not understand the denial, anxiety and absence of services among the professional community.

Priests, ministers and rabbis insisted "that" did not happen among their parishioners. Although there were a few men who did admit "that" was mentioned in the sanctity of the confessional or in private conversation, they felt untrained and unskilled in ways to deal with incestuous assault and seldom attempted counseling or intervention with the members of such troubled families. Pediatricians, other doctors and nurses did not see "that" in their practices, and one young resident in a midwestern city assured me that contrary to all the medical literature I had read, "Seven-year-olds can catch gonorrhea from dirty sheets." Occasionally I found a clinical report of "that" published in a medical journal or a paper presented to a group of psychiatrists by a peer who was working with a sexually abused client. But overwhelmingly I encountered silence.

Such consistent and uniform silence led me to better understand the personal anxiety many professionals bring to their work when they must deal with potentially toxic subjects. I began to see the nature of the self-protection that motivates their separation from both the reality of incestuous assault and the adult family members involved in such abuse. I began to find, too, that this kind of self-protection is employed by all of us in an attempt to shield ourselves from the reality of incestuous behavior.

Until quite recently, incestuous assault cases were seen primarily in the hospitals and police stations of the inner cities across our nation. The people who turn to these institutions for help are lower-class families that have few, if any, alternatives. As a result, the profile of the incest family that emerged did little but reflect the population such institutions most often serve. In turn, this distorted profile kept public concern and attention at arm's length. Incestuous assault was seen as being endemic to seriously disrupted groups of people who display massive pathology in their interpersonal relationships. Many studies that have focused on the lower-class families in our population have highlighted the numbers on public assistance, the children within them born out of wedlock, the degree of drug and chemical dependency of the parents, the high incidence of wife-beating, violent behavior, child abuse and neglect, promiscuity and crowded living quarters. All of these behaviors were seen as corresponding to the incidence of incestuous abuse within these families and many as having precipitated the assault. Over the years there was little, if any, positive intervention or help offered to such families with incestuous abuse problems, and any expression of public outrage included jail for the offender, a foster home for the victim and continued public assistance and scorn for the remaining fragmented family.

Such families have been studied, scrutinized and reduced to statistics while their members continue to stagger under the burdens of being poor and uneducated in a society that has little room or need for them. Many are locked into lives from which they can see no escape, lives that generate enormous frustration and rage and that offer few places to turn to for hope. These men and women have become estranged from themselves, their marriage partners and their work (if they have any), and their frustrations are likely to reach an explosive level. There are few upon whom such powerless people can vent their fury, and their children become prime targets for abuse.

However, it has become increasingly difficult to continue to ascribe the difficult conditions of lower-class life as the source of incestuous assault. Such a simplistic, culture-bound analysis cannot hold up in the face of the growing number of aggressors whose singular characteristic in common is that they sexually assault their own children. They are otherwise as "typical" as you and I. By our insistence that it is only "those people" who assault their children, we can avoid facing the abuse that has been going on around us.

The incest family's need for anonymity coupled with our

inability to imagine that such things occur in our own communities keep the statistics unfairly weighted on the lower classes. The widespread occurrence of incestuous abuse has been clouded by the fact that nearly all cases in middle- and upper-class homes remain unreported and may be revealed only to private psychiatrists or therapists. Among the more affluent, incestuous assault is simply a better-kept secret.

The true range of families dealing with incestuous assault has little to do with class, race, economic status or social background. Were it possible to provide a more realistic profile of a typical family in which incestuous abuse occurs, it would more likely be a middle-class family composed of husband, wife and children living together in a nuclear situation. The adults would be Republicans as often as Democrats, involved in their church and active in community affairs, the same people you and I pass on the street each morning.

As long as we continue to believe that incestuous assault can happen only in other families, we can avoid examining our own lives. As long as we insist upon imagining the incestuous aggressor to be an easily identifiable, skulking, lascivious male who ravishes his luscious and budding daughter across town, we can keep a safe distance. This distance protects us from sexual feelings we may have experienced for older family members and any possible interplay that may have occurred in our own childhood as well as feelings we may have toward our children as we watch them developing into young men and women. While most of us do not act upon these feelings, it is our refusal to acknowledge to ourselves that we have ever had such feelings that creates our silence, aversion and unwillingness to openly discuss the issues involved in incestuous abuse.

We all are familiar with warnings about strangers who offer children rides and candy in order to lure them into secluded settings to molest them. Only infrequently is this the case. Seventy-five percent of all reported sexual abuse of children is committed by someone the victim knows and trusts.[3] And all too frequently that someone is a member of the victim's immediate family.

As upsetting as a sexual assault upon a child can be for a family, it is easier for a parent to rally around the victim when the assailant is a stranger than when the assailant is a relative. Parental anger can be redirected more readily toward supporting the child in his or her shock and confusion, and attention can be focused on apprehending and prosecuting the assailant. But what happens when the assailant is an uncle, older brother or father? In that situation, it is not so easy for family members to clarify priorities and know whom to protect and whom to defend, especially if confronting the offender means that the family unit and its economic foundation will be threatened.

There are many reasons why so few cases of incestuous assault are reported, and these will be more thoroughly discussed in the chapters which follow. But, for a moment, consider these questions: If you were victimized by a parent, whom would you tell? If your child were to tell you of sexual play between herself and your spouse, what would you do? If you found yourself compulsively molesting your children or their playmates, where would you go for help?

There are few communities that have developed uniform, non-punitive reporting laws and family counseling services. There are even fewer alternatives available for families who want help and yet will not report the abuse to the authorities. As a result, the course of action most frequently taken by victims and aggressors alike remains the same. They do nothing, they tell no one and the incestuous behavior remains an awful and hidden secret. Although there are no accurate statistics, most studies to date point to a shattering number of families that are harboring such a secret.

It is estimated that anywhere from fifty to ninety percent

of all sexual assaults upon children remain unreported. In cases in which the assailant is a relative, the closer the relationship of the offender to the child, the less likely that the abuse will be revealed to anyone and the greater the chance that it will continue.

Although the aggressor most often is the victim's father, grandfather, stepfather or uncle, he or she is always an adult whom the child has reason to trust in a loving and intimate situation. Seldom does an aggressor use threats or physical force since rarely is there need to intimidate a child who already trusts the adults in his or her family. Furthermore, physical abuse could lead to discovery of the incest. Most incestuous assault situations involve victims who have participated for a period of years, because in many cases the relationship provides rewards for the child that are not necessarily sexual but fill the child's needs for attention, physical closeness and love.

In 1969, the Children's Division of the American Humane Association completed a study of 1,100 cases of child sexual abuse in the borough of Brooklyn, New York. This organization is committed to the development of better and more creative protective services for children and has worked tirelessly to prevent neglect, abuse and exploitation of children. In its study, the organization found that 75 percent of the offenders were known to the children or their families. Twenty-seven percent were members of the immediate household, and another 11 percent were relatives who were not living in the home. The average age of the children who were victimized was eleven years, and in 41 percent of the families studied the sexual abuse had continued for a period of seven years.[4]

Although the vast majority of incestuous assault cases remain unreported, recent investigations indicate how frequently incest is discovered to be at the root of reported cases of sexual abuse. When the Sacramento, California, sheriff's department investigated 103 cases of sexual molestation of juveniles, they found that 80 of that number were incestuously based.[5] More and more agencies across the country are finding that when they begin to update their intake procedures and develop more sophisticated screening techniques in hospitals, schools and counseling situations, incestuous assault is discovered to be a reality in the lives of thousands of children.

A report written by a Connecticut physician in 1975 indicated that as a result of strengthened reporting statutes for child abuse in that state, along with a proliferation of crisis hotlines serving troubled families, the number of reported cases of incestuous assault in Connecticut jumped from 19 in 1973 to 47 in 1974. During that same year, the total number of cases of suspected child sexual abuse escalated from 669 to nearly 2,000 in that one state.[6] And those figures are believed to be only the tip of the iceberg.

The recent jump in incestuous assault statistics is confirmed in the caseload of the Child Sexual Abuse Treatment Program in San Jose, California. It was the first program of its kind in the country and is designed to work closely with the criminal justice system to provide psychological intervention, counseling, support groups and treatment for all members of the incest family as an alternative to sending the aggressor to prison and disrupting the family and any possibility of its reconstructing itself. The first year of its operation (1971) in a county (Santa Clara) of about a million people, predominately white and middle class, the center worked with thirty incest families. The number of cases was significantly larger than the generally accepted estimate of less than two incest offenders per million population in the United States annually, which was based on a study of incest behavior by Dr. S. Kirson Weinberg published in 1955. Dr. Weinberg's findings of 1.2 incest offenders per million persons in the United States in 1910, 1.9 per million persons in 1920 and 1.1 per million persons in 1930 were used as the accepted statistical base for incest behavior until the early 1970s.[7] His estimate was felt by professionals to be so comfortably low that they turned their attention and resources to what they felt were more frequently occurring family problems.

In Santa Clara, as a result of sensitive nationwide media coverage of their program, the number of families to receive counseling has increased from the original 30 families in 1971 to 600 families having received help by 1977. In one county alone, therefore, the previous estimate of two incest offenders per million is seen to be grossly inaccurate. Hank Giarretto, who founded tne Santa Clara project, believes that when more programs are developed throughout the country to provide the kind of intervention that stresses rebuilding family members rather than punishing and separating them, then we will see more and more families seeking help. Giarretto further believes that sexual abuse of children by immediate family members and other relatives is rising in epidemic proportion. He has been a pioneer in incest trauma counseling and a tireless speaker in urging community leaders across the country to begin developing programs to provide help for incest families caught in non-productive and harmful ways of relating.

But for many communities it is still easier to pay attention to less uncomfortable social problems. There has been local and national acknowledgment of the growing problems of adolescent alcoholism, runaways, drug addiction and suicide. These are issues that can be, and are, openly discussed. Alternatives to incarceration and punishment are developed; meetings and seminars are held; curricula are designed and monies made available to mount an all-out effort at bringing to bear all of our nation's skills, resources and expertise to address these growing problems.

However, perhaps the behaviors we are trying to ameliorate are sometimes symptoms of a deeper and more painful problem. Several retrospective studies would seem to indicate that underlying much of adolescent "acting out" is a deeper source of pain that has been overlooked or ignored. In 1975, the *Runaway Newsletter* identified sexual abuse as one of the three primary reasons children run away from home.[8] In a study conducted in Minneapolis, 75 percent of the women working as prostitutes were found to have been victims of incestuous assault.[9] Interviews held in a Boston hospital with 42 children and adolescents who had been sexually traumatized indicated that half of the offenders were family members, including fathers, grandfathers and stepfathers.[10] The assaults had continued for a period of time because the offenders' access to the children had never been questioned by other family members. And, in New York City, a drug program reported that 44 percent of all female addicts in their rehabilitation center had been incestuously assaulted.[11]

Not all of the studies have been concerned with disturbed and angry victims, however. In a questionnaire sent to 1,800 college students, one-third indicated that they had at some point in their lives been sexually abused.[12] Other studies conclude that 80 percent of all children are victimized by an adult they know and trust.[13]

In searching further for consistent statistics, I discovered an additional dimension of the problem. In the *Uniform Crime Report* published by the FBI, there is no classification of "crimes against the person" according to victims' ages. There is a great deal of information relating to sex offenses and sex offenders, but few ways to correlate that to the sexual abuse of children generally and by family members specifically. Furthermore, the legal language used to define offenses varies greatly; "forcible rape" in one jurisdiction might be considered "impairing the morals of a minor" in another. Added to the confusion of overlapping legal definitions is the option of plea-bargaining by the offender, as well as the victim's or the family's reluctance to press charges and become involved with prosecution which will require the child to testify in court and be subjected to cross-examination. All of these factors affect statistics pertaining to the incidence of incestuous assault in our country.

We don't know how widespread incestuous assault is and can only estimate its true dimensions. Legal statutes that are applicable to sexual abuse of children within their families differ from state to state, and mandatory reporting laws are seldom enforced. However, although the statistics we have are incomplete, confusing and often contradictory, they point to a problem of enormous dimension and implication for the lives of uncounted thousands of young people who carry their secret alone and in silence.

In this book I shall attempt to uncover the dynamics of incestuous assault by presenting personal histories of people who have been involved in such abuse, in the hope that other victims and their families will discover that they are not alone. I am writing, too, for those of us who have had no personal contact with incestuous assault. For while so many of us have difficulty in dealing with our own sexuality and while our understanding of the nature and functioning of our family lives is based upon culturally defined myths, we share similar frustrations and confusion with those families in which sexual assault is manifested. If there is a difference among us, it is in degree, not in kind.

Incestuous assault is a personal and a social problem. By understanding how and why it occurs with such discomforting frequency we can begin to develop programs and alternatives to the ineffective and often contradictory approaches presently taken in most communities. Because of our own unresolved anxieties about family sexuality, we find it extremely difficult to deal clearly and compassionately with the reality of incestuous assault. It is difficult for us to look at the lives of others whose behavior may uncomfortably reflect feelings that lay buried within us. Difficult, and frightening perhaps, but necessary in order for us to come to a deeper understanding of not only the larger problem, but of our own lives.

THE CHILDREN

♦ ♦ ♦ ♦ ♦ ♦ ♦ ♦ ♦ ♦

Carmen

Carmen is a young Latina. Her body is square, chunky, solid. She holds herself tightly, carefully watching every- thing around her with keen eyes, and appears calm and in control.

Carmen barely touched her coffee, kept her hands tightly folded in her lap and moved only slightly during the many hours we spoke together. Several times, when she began to feel upset, her voice became soft, nearly inaudible, and her eyes filled with tears. But her tears were never shed. For years she had not allowed her tears to fall.

"When I was born, my mother was a professor of political science in a small Central American country. Before my first birthday, however, another political group had taken power and she couldn't work in the university any longer. She and my father took me and whatever belongings they could carry and came to America on the first plane that had space.

"Both she and my father were Catholic. Shortly after we arrived, my father died. I don't remember if I ever was told

the children

what caused his death. My mother seldom speaks of him.
On the rare occasions he is mentioned, there is a strain to
her voice that betrays how deeply she must have loved him
and what a loss it was for her when she was left alone in a
strange country with a small child.

"Her faith saw her through those years, as it did during
the many periods of crisis in her life, and she didn't remarry
until I was nearly ten. During all that time, she remained
celibate and taught in a small, Catholic girls' school. We
were very close, and I felt lucky to have such a perfect
mother. Whenever I would listen to the other girls in my
classes at school talk about their mothers, I always privately
felt special.

"When she remarried, I suppose I was jealous of him.
Having to share your mother after all those years of having
her to yourself is hard on kids, and I was no different.

"My stepfather behaved in a seductive way with me from
the very beginning. He would be sweet and thoughtful
when my mother was around, but as soon as she would
leave on Sunday mornings for church, all that would fly
right out the window. He would make me sit with him at
the kitchen table and listen to him go on about his mother,
who had been unfaithful to his father. He had been deeply
attached to his father and would go on and on listing griev-
ances about his mother. He would always end his mono-
logue by making sexual overtures to me. I sort of knew
what he was doing, but had been raised rather strictly and
never knew exactly what to say to him.

"When I was eleven, my mother returned to Central
America to spend the summer with her dying brother. I
was frightened about her being gone for such a long period
of time. I was afraid that I wouldn't be able to hold my
stepfather off and something awful might happen with all
the time we would have alone.

"I was right. Within days after she left, he forced me to have
intercourse with him and continued to do so throughout

19

the entire summer. It wasn't often that it happened, but it was violent and ugly whenever it did.

"I became pregnant. When my mother returned home, I told her that my periods had stopped. That was all I said, and she didn't ask any questions and silently gave me some pills to take to try to bring on my menses. I started the sixth grade taking the pills, participating in all the sports classes, doing everything I could think of to abort the baby. Nothing worked.

"I left school a few weeks before Easter vacation, supposedly to visit a relative, and had the baby. During all those months, my mother assumed I was protecting a neighborhood boy. Being the good Catholic that she was, she decided to keep the baby and raise it as her own son and a brother to the boy she had had with my stepfather the year before.

"When I think back about that time, I really was a schizophrenic. In school I was smart, achieving, the highest honor-roll student the school had ever had. That was the only place I could get the approval I was so hungry for. Being smart seemed to be the best way to get adult approval.

"At home I kept my feelings to myself. That was the only way I could feel any sense of power over the adults in my life. If I never let them know that what they did mattered to me, then they couldn't hurt me. Nobody ever knew what I felt or thought—about anything.

"When my baby was two months old, my stepfather tried to assault me again. This time he threatened me, if I wouldn't let him have intercourse with me. I began to be afraid I would kill him. I kept thinking about the big kitchen knives, just tiptoeing into his room at night after he was asleep and stabbing him all over his body. I was so frightened by my feelings I decided there was nothing I could do but just tell my mother the truth.

"I remember hearing the sound of my own voice in my ears as I told her. It was flat, non-committal, factual—no

emotion at all. I just told her. She sent him away at once, and he was smart enough to know that she meant what she said. If he didn't pack and go, she would call the police. And she would have. I was so proud of her for having done that.

"But, of course, once he left, so did his income. Mother had to quit her job to stay home and care for the two children. I was still in high school, and it felt somehow like my fault that such a bright, perfectionist academic like my mother was stuck in the house with these two little boys. I felt so guilty for her life and tried everything I could to make her proud of me. I got honor-roll grades and would rush home after school every day to shop and clean and work part-time jobs, anything I could think of to try to help out. I carried all the responsibility I could, and then some.

"When I started my final year in high school, I worked full time in a convalescent home and began to put on a lot of weight. My whole last year was spent being top in my class, working full time and becoming increasingly fat.

"When I finally got out of high school, I decided to move and have a chance to make a different life for myself. I spent the next year working two jobs to accumulate the money I needed for a new start.

"I hadn't been away three months when my mother called to say there had been an accident with the baby and I had to return at once. Only after I rushed home did I realize her call had been a ruse and the 'accident' a minor abrasion. She was just lonely and wanted me to be closer to her and the boys.

"I have chosen to stay. My weight still is the central physical manifestation of my incest experiences. All that extra flesh is the separation I need between myself and my sexual feelings. I don't trust my feelings, and if I can keep myself fat and unattractive, I don't need to deal with them at all. I'm smart, funny and people like me. I have decided that

will simply have to be enough. My weight also is the source of my power and protection against feeling small and vulnerable, like I was as a skinny little kid of eleven.

"I do have some relationships with men. Usually the men are older intellectuals, where there are few sexual expectations. Sometimes they are gay men, and infrequently they are bisexual men whose own sexual confusions preclude their making any demands on me. That way I can enjoy the company of men but don't have to deal with the sexuality inherent in having intimate relationships with them.

"I suppose the hardest part for me, still, is trying to talk openly with my mother about the incest. When I try to bring it up, she begins to cry and blame herself for it having happened. She feels that she chose him, and whatever he did is her responsibility. What I keep trying to make her understand, and what is still unresolved, is that my mother and I shared this experience together. I don't want us to be separated by any feeling that what happened was her fault or mine. It wasn't. It was his fault, and until we can both accept that, we can never have the kind of relationship we had together before he came into our lives."

Gene

It began for Gene thirteen years ago, when he was five. At eighteen, Gene's face and manner of speaking are the same as those of other young men from comfortable, middle-class homes in suburban neighborhoods, but he is one of the many who permitted me to hear their pain, guilt, shame—and finally their outrage—at having been sexually abused.

I visited Gene in the adolescent psychiatric ward of a large city hospital, where he had been admitted a year earlier after he had tried to kill himself by slashing open both his wrists. The wounds on his arms healed far more rapidly than those hidden in his mind and heart. Gene is beginning to show signs of progress, but on his ward and hundreds of similar wards around the country there are a thousand other boys like him.

I have talked with Gene and you will hear his story. But who is there to see and hear and help the countless others?

"The first time I really remember was when I was eight years old. A friend had given me a copy of Playboy magazine, and I took it into my bedroom to look at it. My father came into the room while I had the magazine open, and he sat down on the bed so we could look at it together.

"A lot of the things he was saying about the women in the pictures made me uncomfortable. After a few minutes, when he noticed I had an erection, he reached down and touched it. My erection got even bigger when he did that, and he began to fondle me, and finally he took my penis out of my pants and made love to me orally and had me do the same to him.

"I felt shocked and guilty and confused because what he did felt so good. I knew what we had done was wrong, but I had let him do it and there wasn't any way I could tell anyone about what had happened. I was afraid people would think I was bad.

"We had sex like that a few times a month, whenever he would find me alone in the house. It was always his idea, but I never said that I didn't want to. It got so that each time made it harder and harder for me to stop it from happening, and I wished even stronger it had never begun at all.

"By the time I got into junior high, my father and I were having all kinds of sex together, and it got so that I dreaded every time I knew my mother and sisters would be gone for the day. I tried every excuse I could to keep out of the house so I wouldn't have to be alone with him.

"There was no one I could tell because I was afraid nobody would believe me. So I kept quiet. All through junior high school it was on my mind nearly all the time. I was thinking about the sex, thinking about why there was a

*part of me that enjoyed it, wondering whether anybody
would find out at school, worrying what my mother would
do if she ever knew about it. It got so I could hardly think
about anything else. My grades were never very good
because I couldn't seem to concentrate on my work, and
as you can tell by looking at me, I'm not the athletic type
and never felt I could try out for sports.*

*"When I entered tenth grade, there was an older boy who
was just going into his senior year. He was like me in a lot
of ways. He was pretty quiet and shy and not very popular.
He became my first real friend.*

*"My friend and I used to spend a lot of time together
after school and on the weekends, just doing regular
things. We went to the movies and some rock concerts and
smoked some dope. He was so kind and always seemed to
be interested in whatever I wanted to talk to him about. It
never seemed to be important what subject I was talking
about, he always made me feel that what I said mattered.
Who I was mattered. You could really say that he was the
first person I ever really loved.*

*"I was spending less and less time in the house because all
my spare time was spent with my friend. My father began
to question me closely about who my new friend was and
where he lived and what we did together. He was acting
jealous about my having a friend. It was as though he
wanted me all to himself.*

*"My friend and I never had sex together, although there
were a few moments when I felt it might have happened.
But he wasn't sure, and I didn't want to. I never said anything to him about what had been going on between me
and my father, and I didn't want to start the same things
with anybody else. I just didn't want to deal with my body
or my feelings about my body at all.*

*"Most of the time I felt sure that having sex with my
father meant I was gay, but as much as I liked my friend
and wanted to be with him all the time, my mind was*

the children

really mixed up. When I would have dreams at night—wet
dreams, I mean—and would have fantasies about sex, I
never thought about boys. It was always girls I would
dream about. It got so that I didn't know whether I was
straight or gay or bisexual or just all around mixed up.

"My dad started coming down on my case all the time
about my relationship with my friend. Things got so bad
with my lying to my dad and lying to my friend I thought
I was starting to go crazy. That was when I decided that I
had to run away. I thought I could go to a place where no
one knew me and I could just figure out who I was and
not have anyone tell me what to do. So I waited one night
until the house was quiet, put some of my clothes in a
paper bag, took all the money I had saved and left.

"By the time I got to the bus station, it was cold and late
and I was tired. I just sat on the bench trying to look like
I was going somewhere, so I wouldn't look suspicious,
and waited until morning. I got on the first bus that pulled
in and ended up in a city a few hundred miles away. I
never really thought about what I was going to do once I
got there—it was just a desperate feeling of wanting to get
away. To go somewhere, anywhere, to a place where
fathers didn't make their own sons have sex with them. Sex
was the absolutely last thing I wanted to get involved with.

"I walked around a lot when I first got to the city. There
were lots of guys my age on the street, and it didn't take
me long to figure out what they were there for. After two
weeks of trying to get a job, any job, and having everyone
say I was too young or too inexperienced or too something—and never hearing anything but 'Sorry' or 'No' or
'Come back again in a few years'—I ended up doing exactly
what I was running from.

"My money was gone, and I couldn't see any way out. I
was hungry and broke and scared and knew I couldn't go
anywhere near home because people were looking for me.
So one night I let a guy take me to a hotel. It really wasn't

awful. It wasn't anything my father hadn't done a hundred times. In fact, it wasn't anything like how it could have been. It was the fastest ten dollars I'd ever made.

"I spent six months working the streets. There were always enough men—usually about my father's age—anxious to buy me clothes and food and give me money besides. I just didn't let myself feel anything all the time it was going on. It was as though every day just happened and there wasn't anything to be done or thought about it.

"After I'd been working about six months, there was a police sweep of the street where I made my contacts, and about twenty of us wound up at juvenile hall. All the feelings of being scared that I had kept buried for months came out when I got to that place. I knew I just couldn't go back home and have my father try sex with me anymore.

"I asked if there was somebody I could talk to about my case, and they took me into a little room with a man and a woman and I told them about me and my father. It was very hard to say it out loud for the first time, and I don't even remember exactly what I said. I guess it just came blurting out.

"Finally I noticed how really strange their faces had gotten, and the guy was clearing his throat a lot and just making marks on his yellow pad. Neither of them were looking at me, though the lady would glance at me and then quickly look away. When I stopped, it got real quiet in the room, and then they said for me to wait and they would be right back.

"A few minutes later another man came in and asked me if what I had said was the truth. I told him yes, and he said he had traced my father and had found out he was the owner of a store and a deacon in our church and an umpire for the Little League. He told me what I had said was a terrible thing to say about 'a man like your father.'

"He told me my parents had been notified and were on their way to pick me up and take me home. Then he assured

*me he wouldn't repeat the 'dreadful lies' I had said about
my dad and that what I had said would stay a secret as
long as I understood how terrible it was that I would even
think, much less say, 'things like that' about my father.*

*"Then the man scraped his chair back from the desk and
said that I would be staying the night upstairs in the dorm-
itory and my parents would pick me up in the morning. He
nodded to let me know the interview was over, and a
matron came to take me upstairs. By that time my head
was pounding so hard I was sure everyone in the place
could hear it, and I thought I was going to throw up.*

*"There was no point in living in a world where I couldn't
change anything—where I was going to have to go home, to
a place where everybody would know I had run away, to
a home where my father would try to have sex with me—
and in a world where I didn't have anybody.*

*"That night I got a razor and tried to cut off my skin.
I wanted to destroy the thing that had caused me all the
trouble and confusion and hurt—my body. I don't remember much after that, until I woke up here."*

*Gene has had an advantage most young victims like him
may never have—the staff at his hospital are aware of, and
sensitive to, the many forms of abuse and trauma experienced by young people who have been involved in incestuous relationships. With help and support available to
him, Gene will no longer be counted in the growing number of male and female incest victims who turn to prostitution, drug abuse, alcoholism or suicide as a means of
obliterating their feelings of grief, frustration and betrayal.*

Who are the victims of incestuous assault? If asked, a number of us might feel we know. Some of us might point our
fingers at poor families—people who have too many children

and too little money and who live crowded together in small rooms in impoverished ghetto areas or in isolated rural communities. Others might describe the victims as teenage girls who are seductive with their fathers and other men. Many of us would assert that the victims directly or indirectly bring on the assaults or that they fantasize or exaggerate their experiences out of proportion.

I seldom found any of the above to be true. Victims are white, black, Latin and Asian. They are male and female. They are five, seven and twelve years old. They are fat, skinny, ugly, beautiful, poor, wealthy and middle class. Incest is relentlessly democratic.

As I traveled and spoke with victims of incestuous assault, I found few people who fit into our stereotypic image of the incest family. Instead:

· I met a six-year-old girl who had caught venereal disease from her father.

· I met a seven-year-old girl who regularly had been forced to masturbate her father when he'd return from a round of golf at his private club.

· I learned of eight-year-olds used as models for pornographic pictures taken by their fathers in expensively equipped home studios.

· I spoke with a nine-year-old who was skilled at practicing fellatio on Daddy in one of the family's guest rooms.

· I met ten-year-old girls and boys who had been forcibly sodomized by their fathers.

· I spoke with an eleven-year-old who, before entering junior high school, was aborted of her father's child.

· I spoke with twelve-year-old girls who are using drugs or alcohol to mask and deny the emotional pain of having been sexually abused by a family member.

· I met teenagers who have become truant from school and who repeatedly run away from home, young people trying to survive on the streets of our cities whose greatest fear is of being caught and returned to the homes from which they fled. I met others who are prostituting their bodies for nameless adults to earn the only livelihood they can and to gratify their need to be cared for, however detached and ephemeral their sexual contacts may be.

These young people are not visible to the agencies that could provide intervention and help alleviate their pain and confusion while they are still living in troubled family situations. Too often, society acts only after a young person's hopelessness, rage and loss of self-esteem have led him or her to behave in ways we find offensive. And then we whisk these youngsters off the streets and punish them. Rather than asking or listening to young people, rather than trying to understand what has precipitated their desperate responses to their family situations, we frequently respond by returning them to their homes—presumed havens—from which they often are literally running for their lives. Or else we place them in institutions that further exploit and victimize them.

Incest victims initially are betrayed by the adults in their families who fail to provide them with emotional, physical and sexual safety, and they are further victimized by a society that shuts its doors and its eyes at the mention of sexual abuse.

Child victims who are coerced with physical threats or force make up only a small percentage of incestuous assault cases. Rarely is it necessary to intimidate a child who already is trusting and open to the adults in his or her family environment. And when physical threats are made, they are seldom carried out; for the aggressor wants the child to be available and silent, and physically harming the child might very well result in detection of the aggressor's offenses.

The majority of cases I observed involved victims who had participated in an ongoing incestuous relationship over a period of years partly because of the rewards, not necessarily sexual, that were offered to them. Although some children are offered money and gifts, most are exploited in a much more subtle manner. They are pressured into sexual activity by adults who are in a kinship relation to them, in a position of power over them, either through age, authority or both, and who are able to take advantage of a child's inability to make or understand sexual decisions. In these cases, the child victim's attitude remains ambivalent. Each of the young men and women with whom I spoke intuitively sensed that the adult's behavior, whether explicit sexual contact or not, "felt funny." But in the words of one young girl, "You are taught that what grownups say and do is right, and even if you feel confused about it, you do what they tell you."

These children submerge their true feelings, distrust their perceptions and deny their own reality. They tell no one about the relationship and behave as though nothing is happening. The tacit consent they appear to give by keeping silent does not preclude feelings of deep uncertainty and confusion. They are fearful of discovery and whatever might be the result of others "knowing."

Debbie, a fifteen-year-old victim, told me, "I used to get extra things from Daddy for being nice to him. He told me never to tell anybody and he would keep on giving me things, like extra spending money. I was only nine when he started, and I liked getting those presents. I didn't like what I had to do to get them, but it was the only spending money I ever got. He never hurt me, and it didn't take too long, so I would just not let myself think it was happening at all. After a while I started to worry all the time and was afraid of anybody finding out. But I had let it go on for so many years without telling anyone, I was afraid people would think it was my fault. So I never told. I just became withdrawn and didn't make friends and tried to stay by myself all the time."

Although nearly all the child victims with whom I spoke sensed that what the adult was doing wasn't right, in many cases it was the only form of love, affection and attention these youngsters were getting. Some felt repulsion or misgivings at once, while others continued in the relationship for years before realizing something was terribly wrong. Sara, a woman in her middle twenties who has spent the past three years in therapy trying to rebuild her sense of self-esteem, told me, "I didn't even know that it didn't happen in everybody's family. Daddy told me it was natural and he was just teaching me the facts of life. I never knew that he wasn't telling me the truth. He had books and everything, used diagrams and made me learn the parts of the body. It wasn't until I was in fifth grade that I began to understand that everybody's daddy didn't do that."

Rita, who is now married and raising her own family, talked about another dimension of this confusion: "When I was small, I never thought to get angry at Daddy. He was very gentle and kind while he was touching me. He never hurt me, and it usually felt nice. I was just utterly mystified about him touching me that way."

When a young girl's father is behaving in a non-violent manner in his sexual contact with her, although the sexual behavior is inappropriate, it can serve to make the victim feel close and loved. Her needs for human contact and warmth become translated into the specific sexual form of her father's stroking and fondling. In a home in which the only love and tenderness a girl receives takes the form of sexual play, the child's slowly growing sense of the wrongness of such intimacy takes years to surface and, when it does, is coupled with her own incorporated feelings of guilt and responsibility for having let it go on.

In many situations in which the father is the aggressor, the eldest daughter is the first to be victimized, and earliest sexual contact can begin when the child is as young as five or six, with genital fondling, mutual masturbation and oral-genital contact frequently reported by victims as their earliest sexual experiences. Such activity is not always traumatic and frightening at the time it occurs if the father is not physically abusive, because he is able to count on his daughter's inability to understand the inappropriateness of his behavior and the warmth and sensual feelings his fondling generates in her. Explicit genital intercourse frequently does not begin until the girl reaches puberty and only after a long history of other sexual play between child and adult. When sexual activity continues for years, the child feels a deepening responsibility to keep the relationship hidden from everyone, and her father is free to escalate the level of sexuality between them.

Money and gifts are no longer appropriate leverage when a child begins to feel that what is happening is wrong. However, even though a young girl may feel partly responsible for the situation and may want to ask for help, she still may refrain from telling anyone and thus remain charged with the secret of her father's behavior. Her silence is based on some very real fears. If she tells, as one woman explained to me, "Daddy said he would punish me. He never said exactly how he would do that, but I believed him." Other women who had been child victims confirmed this fear of punishment, not only by their fathers, but by their mothers, their schools and the police. Although the nature of the punishment was unclear to them, most of the girls, particularly those from religious families, clearly sensed that the weight of the adult world's wrath and the blame would fall solely on them for having been so "bad."

Other women told of having kept the secret for fear of repercussions that would involve their entire family. As one woman put it, "I promised Daddy I would do it with him if he promised not to touch my little sisters like that. He did promise, although I found out years after I left home that he began with them the very day I left." Another woman, who had grown up in an economically marginal family in a large northwestern city, explained:

the children

"My father told me that if I ever let anyone know what he had been doing with me, that the police would send him to jail. Living in my neighborhood, all of us kids knew what kind of place jail was, and I knew if Daddy went there we would have to go on welfare and Mom just wouldn't have been able to keep things together."

A woman from an affluent suburban family cited yet another reason for keeping silent: "Nobody would have believed me. Daddy was a big executive. He was a member of the Community Chest, the Rotary Club and always had his picture in the newspaper. I never felt anyone would believe a kid saying anything like that. I didn't feel I had anyplace to turn and just waited for the day I turned sixteen so I could leave all of them behind me."

Confused, humiliated and in a state of disbelief, child victims often are helpless to disengage themselves. Sadly, because they think that no one will believe them, or will care even if they do believe them or, most painfully, that the relationship is somehow their fault, they continue to accept what often is the only expression of closeness and attention they receive. Such victims feel they have no recourse. Having no way to deal with their fears and anxieties, they sentence themselves to the prison of abuse from which they can see no escape.

Other victims feel that the abuse is condoned, even encouraged, in their families and become immobilized. Arlene, a young woman from a large Italian family, explained: "Daddy used to make me sit on his lap all the time, and he used to rub up against me with his thing all hard until he got all red in the face and would very abruptly push me down. I was only seven when he started to do that, and I still don't understand why nobody ever told him not to do that. It seemed as though my mother must have known he was doing it. Even when my grandfather, Daddy's father, would come to visit on Sundays, he would lean over to kiss me and stick his tongue in my mouth. It was disgusting, that nasty old man, but my mother and father would be standing right there, watching and smiling. So who was I supposed to tell? It never seemed as though anybody cared that that was happening to me."

Other victims told me of the awful estrangement they felt from their brothers and sisters, who sensed they were getting special attention from their parents. Although these siblings usually were younger and did not understand the nature of the attention, they felt shortchanged and became jealous and resentful of the victim, thereby exacerbating the victim's feeling of isolation within the family. In their estrangement, child victims walk a tenuous line between feeling powerful because they hold the key to the secret that keeps their families intact and feeling utterly powerless to find a way to make the abuse stop. They are left carrying the burden of the family secret.

Whether these victims are afraid of being punished by one or both of their parents, afraid of the repercussions to the family system if they tell, afraid of not being believed, afraid of losing the only love and attention they are getting, however anxiety-producing it is, or whether they've come to blame themselves for what has taken place, the secret remains safe with them, and the family closes further in on itself.

Public and professional opinion is fairly consistent in response to the female victims of incestuous assault. A very young girl elicits feelings of protectiveness and outrage. However, if the victim is a fully developed adolescent, our own discomfort with the victim's often sexually aggressive behavior leads many of us to view her as seductive and as having taken advantage of a weak older male. Furthermore, if the victim expresses her pain through drug abuse, alcohol dependency or prostitution, we conclude that she must have been a bad kid all along and must be held at least partially responsible for her situation.

These victims, rightfully disappointed and angry with

their families, become further disillusioned. The professional community—those we would like to believe have the skill and understanding to help victims extricate themselves from sexual abuse—has failed them. Professionals are inadequately trained to deal with the reality of incestuous assault. Many are uncomfortable with the sexually abused child and uncertain how to counsel him or her. I will take a closer look at the professional community in the chapter "The Professional Family," but I would like to make one point here. It is not uncommon for psychiatrists, psychologists, social workers, counselors and mental health workers to see victims as having brought much of their abuse on themselves by having evinced "seductive behavior."

This attitude has been expressed by psychologists in an analysis that further blames children for their own victimization:

> . . . these children undoubtedly do not deserve completely the cloak of innocence with which they have been endowed by moralists, social reformers and legislators. The history of the relationship in our cases usually suggested at least some cooperation of the child in the activity, and in some cases the child assumed an active role in initiating the relationship. . . . It is true that the child often rationalized with excuses of fear of physical harm or the enticement of gifts, but these were obviously secondary reasons. Even in the cases in which physical force may have been applied by the adult, this did not wholly account for the frequent repetition of the practice. . . . Finally, a most striking feature was that these children were distinguished as unusually charming and attractive in their outward personalities. Thus, it is not remarkable that frequently we considered the possibility that the child might have been the actual seducer rather than the one innocently seduced.[1]

Such distortion of motives and culpability continues to

perpetuate the myth of the seductive child rather than focusing attention on the responsibility of the adult to set appropriate limits on acceptable child/adult contact. What appears to be seductive behavior often is a response learned from the adults in a child's life. A child will use whatever behaviors are available to him or her to elicit positive responses from grownups or to get special attention or praise from them.

The child-as-seducer charge is especially damaging to female incest victims. Our culture teaches young girls, implicitly and explicitly, that seductive behavior is a way to get what they want. Acting cute or sexy, even when they are quite young, garners compliments and attention. Furthermore, a girl's socialization teaches her at the same time to internalize guilt for such learned behavior. Therefore female incest victims in effect have been preprogrammed to blame themselves—they feel they must have done something "bad" to have caused the abuse to happen. This became startlingly clear to me when a young man I was interviewing, who had been sexually abused by his uncle when he was ten, explained how it made him feel: "I felt dirty, disgusting and nasty. Just like a girl." In his view, that was the clearest way to define being a victim—being just like a girl. The responsibility for so dangerously shifting the accountability for incestuous behavior onto the female victim rests squarely on the patriarchal nature of our society as a whole and makes us aware of the double victimization and powerlessness of being a child and a girl.

In cases where an adult male has, for whatever reason, chosen to eroticize his relationship with a girl child, the socialization process for females has taught the child to deny the angry, aggressive and rebellious feelings his behavior generates in her. Female incest victims suppress such feelings about the inappropriateness of the adult males' behavior and are thus doubly victimized. They are not only victims of parents who are unable to provide genuine and supportive models of adult behavior, but also are victims of a society that holds them responsible for the actions of adults and will not permit them to be angry and insist on their right to their own bodies. They are expected to internalize their angry feelings and accept the fate adult males hand them.

Child victims, coerced into repressing their feelings and keeping silent about the incestuous relationships thrust upon them, often give us non-verbal clues to the pain they are experiencing. By the time preschool victims enter grade school, their need to tell, whether conscious or unconscious, takes many disparate forms of expression. One female counselor told me sadly, "I had an eight-year-old girl who would constantly find reasons to come into my office and would rub herself suggestively and sexually against my leg, looking up into my face all the while. I was quite discomforted by her behavior and, more sharply than I should have, told her to stop doing that. I never once stopped to wonder where she had learned to do that. Had I been less uncomfortable and more open to what she was trying to tell me, I might have been able to save her from further abuse."

Many child victims, labeled as having learning disorders, expend little concentration on their classwork because keeping their secret takes so much of their energy. Arlene, victimized by both her father and grandfather, remembered, "I felt so different from the other kids in school. I was sure that if I wasn't careful they would be able to tell about me. I was sure I was going to give it away by something I might say or do in school. I was very careful to be quiet, never raise my hand and not draw any attention to myself. I never even laughed out loud until just a few years ago. I tried to be invisible."

Not all victimized children limit themselves to withdrawn and passive behavior. Some victims choose more explicit methods of trying to tell us their secrets. A teacher told me about one of her students who drew a stick figure of an enormous man with a large pole coming out of his stomach. From the end of the pole was a spray of what the girl described as "snot." The teacher remembered the child being called into the principal's office, berated for her artwork and warned never to draw such things again. Other children are punished for pulling up their skirts, teaching others how to masturbate either themselves or boys, or compulsively explaining to all in earshot how babies are made.

After the early signals—either changes in the child's behavior or specific expressions of uncomfortably precocious sexual knowledge—have gone unheeded, many victims begin to experience an overwhelming feeling of having been betrayed, not only by the sexual aggressor but also by other family members and adults who have failed to recognize and stop the abuse. By this time, irrevocable damage has been done to a child's developmental process, and there is insufficient ego strength available for the victim to cope with the frustration, rage and conflict sexual abuse generates. These feelings heighten the already significant loss of self-esteem and the unresolved grief and anger felt by the victim and precipitate, in adolescence, the urgent need to find relief from the burden of his or her secret, resulting in what professionals label "anti-social" behavior.

Since the adults in the homes of incest victims cannot answer their needs for warmth, closeness and affection in a non-sexual manner, disruptive, rebellious or totally withdrawn youngsters are the inexorable result of the disappointment such lack of nurturing generates. These children have to deal not only with the incestuous abuse and the weight of the secret, but also with the denial that such abuse can occur. One victim explained: "You come to believe that you're the crazy one and take all the responsibility for what is happening. It seems clear that nobody wants to hear about it. You try lots of different ways to tell, and nobody is listening. So you stop trying and come to the only conclusion that seems left to you. That it's you that is bad, and that if you hadn't been so bad, Daddy wouldn't have had sex with you."

Furthermore, despite the emotional poverty within a victim's family, it is still the only family the child has and risks losing if he or she divulges the abuse. In the words of another victim, "Little kids still need the idea of a family, even if they never really had one. If you tell, you'll be left with no family at all."

The price of keeping the secret, of protecting themselves and their families, escalates as the victims reach adolescence and often explodes in a multitude of behavior patterns that, if closely examined, can be seen to reflect the loss and pain these youngsters are feeling.

"Men only want you to get them off." This statement was made by a young woman who has worked as a prostitute for the past ten years. She looked considerably older than her twenty-three years and spoke in a tired voice. In the absence of a loving and protective father who cared for her in a non-sexual way while she was growing up, this woman drew the conclusion many victims do. She ran away from home at fifteen, went to a large eastern city and immediately became involved with a man like her father, except that he was a pimp.

The young woman was more than willing to explain and rationalize her choices to me: "He provides the function of father/lover, except he doesn't beat me like my own father did. In many ways he is the father I never had. He loves me and cares about my well-being. He is the only man who ever has. The sex has nothing to do with it. I learned when I was still a kid that sex has nothing to do with anything except how you can learn to use it to get you what you want. My 'daddy' understands that the same way I do, and our relationship is based on the fact that we love and care for each other."

conspiracy of silence

On that note, the young woman signaled that the interview was over and that she had to return to work. As she returned to the street, I understood but was saddened by her need to believe that what she was sharing with her pimp had anything to do with love. She is not really a girlfriend, but a dependent daughter, and is exchanging her sexual services with a series of strangers to please the man who pretends to play the role of the father she still needs.

Not surprisingly, a pimp is protected in many of the same ways that an incestuous father is. A hooker will not testify against her pimp. Even though he may be uncaring, abusive or unkind to her, he is the only love and protection she has. Teenage runaways, particularly those from sexually abusive homes, want someone to touch them and have physical contact with them; that is the only expression of love they understand. The pimp recognizes this need and gives his women the feeling of belonging they may never have received from their families.

A recent federal study estimated that 260,000 youngsters aged seventeen or younger ran away from home for more than a week in 1975, which is triple the number reported in 1964.[2] This is another in the barrage of signals that many youngsters are taking the only option they feel they have. In the same way that a person's sexuality is grounded in his or her early home life, the roots of a young person's prostitution may be found there as well.

A counselor in a northwestern city, who was herself a victim of incestuous assault, a drug user and a prostitute, is angered by the public's inability to see the underlying causes of young prostitutes' behavior. When a child has been sexually abused at an early age, sex becomes a survival skill, a way to get what she or he needs. The counselor explained that a young female victim may learn that if she has sex with Dad tonight, she will get to go out on the weekend. Even before puberty a girl often learns to use her sexuality to please her father. After several years she may see prostitution as a logical extension of selling sex at home. Many abused women decide that if they have to have sex with a man, they might as well get paid for it. Some, who have never learned the difference between sex and love, may repeatedly trade their sexuality for the only touching and affection they have ever received. Many cannot permit themselves to experience the rage they feel at their fathers for having abused them and pick other men who will abuse them further; for if they were to permit the possibility to surface that all men are not like their fathers, the loss would be too difficult to bear. Therefore, in choosing men who will behave much as their fathers did, they displace their rage at their fathers onto the whole community of men, having repeated and meaningless sex with them in a futile attempt to confirm that "they are all alike."

It is important to recognize that not all juvenile runaways and prostitutes are female. In a recently published book about boy prostitutes, the author suggests that there are nearly 300,000 boys working the streets.[3] Many who have studied this phenomenon believe that a large percentage of these young male prostitutes have opted for life "on the streets" primarily as a result of having been sexually abused in their homes.

But prostitution is only one of the signals incest victims give us. A woman who lives in a southern city told me of her experiences:

"I was the oldest one of four children. Daddy forced me to have sex with him when I was only nine. We lived in a small country town, and everybody in it was afraid of him. When nobody was around, he used to make me go up into the hayloft with him. He would tear my panties off and have intercourse with me. My mother always seemed distant, and I didn't feel I could tell her what Daddy was doing. I tried to keep out of everybody's way and find chores to do that kept me out of reach.

conspiracy of silence

"When I was in third grade, my teacher tried to rub my stomach and chest whenever he could get me alone. That went on during the entire school year, and I decided that men were like that and it was best to stay away from them. The only fun I had was with my little brother. He was really my only friend. When I was in sixth grade he was killed in a car accident. Then nothing mattered.

"I was sad and lonesome for my brother, but it came out in acting bad. I started to skip school, my grades got real low and the principal kept threatening to expel me. I didn't care about any of it.

"I started stealing things from town. A shiny pink comb and mirror set, postcard pictures of places that were far away and money if I could get into somebody's pocket-book. I was going to save up and get different clothes and go to a big city. I had almost seventy dollars hidden in my pillow when Daddy found it and took it away from me.

"Finally I met a boy in high school who liked me and said I was pretty. I let him do it with me. Being with him wasn't different than with my father. It was all pretty quick, and he didn't even look at me the whole time. But I got pregnant. Daddy and Mother said I had brought disgrace on the family and had to get out.

"I went to _____ and got on welfare. I got a small place, and I kept it real clean and nice, with daisies on the table and everything. But when the baby was eight months old, I was giving him a bath and found myself touching him on his private parts, and I got scared that I was going to do the same thing to him that Daddy had done to me. It was just awful to think of touching my baby that way. I never let myself do that again, but that was the start of my using drugs. It's like that day changed everything for me. When I was high I could keep away from people, stay close and private with myself so nobody would know how awful I was. I just stayed around the house, cleaning, cooking, getting high and just sitting. It made me feel safe.

the children

"When the child welfare people reported me as being an unfit mother, it was like my life was over. First my brother and now my son, the only two people who ever meant anything to me. Both of them gone.

"A woman in the welfare office told me about a group where you could go and talk about your life. Even though I didn't think anybody would be able to help me, I didn't have anything more to lose at that point, so I went.

"I feel now that I understand a lot of what happened to me, and the women in the group are helping me try to get my son back. I have a job and a nice apartment that I share with some other women. I have a chance to start again, and I only wish that there were more groups in every city so women like me could go and talk with people before their situations become as bad as mine did."

In counseling groups that are beginning to be organized throughout the country, incest victims are encouraged to share their experiences with each other. Such groups serve several invaluable functions. Group members are encouraged to relate their experiences, knowing they will be believed, so that they can move into more positive patterns of living; for it is in the act of defusing the past that victims can begin to reconstruct their lives. Furthermore, while members are resolving their painful experiences, the group provides them with much needed emotional support.

I was invited to sit in on a meeting held by a group of women who had been incestuously assaulted as children. Although the specific experiences and responses of the group members varied, the lack of and consequent longing for good parenting was the underlying thread in each of their lives. Many spoke of their fear of men, of wanting to reach out to men with love, with caring, but without sex. These women felt powerless to find a way to incorporate their own damaged sexuality into loving relationships. The fear of sexuality caused many to feel emotionally raped during intercourse; for others, all touching was so weighted with painful memories that they were unable to feel a closeness with and freedom to touch their own children.

One woman, who has been married for seven years to a loving man who is aware of her early experiences with her father, explained her confusion: "I love Jim and want to make him happy. But when we start to make love and he wants me to do things to him that were the same things I had to do to my Dad, I simply freeze. Part of me is that little girl who has finally found the strength to say no to her father, and the other part of me feels guilty that I am making my husband suffer for the experiences of my past. I feel trapped and drowning in my own history."

Many of the group members are living in an emotional vacuum, fearful of repeated wounding and fearing sex itself beyond their search for an appropriate context in which to place it. Their specific fear results from the disproportionate size of the sexual organs that were forced into their yet undeveloped child bodies. "I felt like I was being ripped up the middle from my legs all the way to my throat," remembered one woman. "I was sure that if I opened my eyes and looked down, I would be in two parts on the bed." Unable to continue, the woman was held and gently rocked by two other women in the group until she was able to compose herself and let the memory of her rape fade, at least for the moment. "I know just how you feel," another woman volunteered. "I have never experienced pain like that in my life before or since, and I bled for days afterward."

One woman stayed with me after the meeting had ended. As we sat together talking, she tried to help me understand. She was young, scrubbed and wholesome looking, but her eyes revealed her pain. "We create our own denial system," she explained. "We erect a wall between us and what has happened. There are lots of ways to build that wall—drugs, alcohol, whatever brings immediate oblivion will serve. If people could only find a way to look past that wall, they might understand that many of our choices are the only ways we know to survive."

Another woman came back into the room and told me of the reactions her incest experiences triggered. "When I was in sixth grade, I came to school with cigarette burns all over my left arm. I had done it because I was feeling scared that I was beginning not to feel anything. I needed to see if I was still real, if I could still hurt. So I burned myself and came to school the next day wearing a short-sleeved dress so that everyone would see. They sent me to the principal, who told me that was a bad, dangerous thing to do. He sent me home and said I had to stay there till it healed."

In a midwestern city, a middle-aged woman told me about the sexual relationship she had had with her step-father from the time she was five until she was eleven. Her emotional confusion led to her becoming truant, defiant and aggressive toward all authority. Finally she was placed in a foster home. "Be sure you talk about foster homes," she said firmly. "There is as much sexual abuse going on there as in so-called real families. Why do you think many of these people want to be foster parents anyway? It's a source of cheap labor for them, and we are their property. They can do anything with us that they want to, just like real parents."

I mentioned this conversation to another woman who had spent most of her childhood in a series of foster homes, and she helped me understand a corollary to that experi-ence: "When they found out about Daddy, they put me in a foster home right away. My foster family was good to me and tried to help me, but I couldn't let them, because it would have meant that they would become my family. Then I would have had to admit that I really didn't have a family of my own. As soon as I felt myself starting to care for them, I would do something bad so I'd have to leave and go to another home."

Learning to understand and forgive a non-protective

mother proves difficult for many victims. I spoke with a
woman in a small New England college town who described
this painful process. Peggy was continually abused by her
father from the time she was nine until she was able to
run away from home at sixteen. On her father's scorecard
she was only one of many women.

"My dad used to run around all the time with low wom-
en," Peggy recalled, "and I knew my mother knew about
it. He never even tried to keep it a secret. He used to say
that she had driven him to other women. When I was
younger, I used to feel sorry for him because my mother
was so cold. Not only to him, but to us kids, too. She
spent all her time alone in the back of the house watching television or sewing funny little costumes for dolls she
collected from different parts of the world. She had quite
a collection of those dolls. I never felt I could tell her
about what Daddy was doing to me because I knew she
hated him for being with other women. You could see that
by the way she looked at him. I was afraid that if I told,
she might hate me, too. She finally divorced him, after her
mother died and left her a little money. The reason she
gave was all his other women. That made me feel terrible,
like I was one of his other women. I was competing with
my own mother."

Peggy went on to tell me about her years on the street,
her search for a man to love and protect her and her decision to enter a therapy group run by feminists in the town
in which she lives. The group helped her to place her
anger appropriately on her father and to begin open communication with her mother.

"When my mother and I started to talk about it, I discovered that she, too, had been molested when she was
small, by both her father and older brother," Peggy continued. "Somehow, Mother found herself married to a man
who was just like her father. She simply couldn't handle it
and withdrew into her own childhood, the one she never

had. She didn't understand all that herself until I got her to come to the group with me. We are pretty good friends now. She's become a traditional grandma, always bringing presents and games to my daughter. It gives me such pleasure to watch them together. My child is getting what neither of us ever had."

Other women are not so forgiving of their mothers. In an explosion undiminished by the passage of years, a victim told me, "I never actually told her what my father was doing, but my God, the laundry could have! There were bloody panties, semen-stained pajamas, soiled sheets. Everything was right there for her to see. And she chose not to."

An older woman said, "I always felt my mother was pushing me on my father. I was the one who had to be sure he had dinner when he got home from work. I was the one who did all the laundry. I was the one who had to sit with him in the evenings while she went into her room and watched television." In such a situation, the female victim feels compelled to assume her mother's role, internalize her own anger and confusion and never reveal the secret that could disband her family. It is an enormous weight to place on the narrow shoulders of a young child. The victim intuits what is required of her to keep her family together, and she will do so, even at the price of her continued victimization.

Furthermore, child victims who take on the task of mothering their mothers have no source within the family to which they can turn for their emotional needs. As another victim explained to me, "When Mom came back from the hospital after her hysterectomy, she just lay around looking at the ceiling. Dad used to complain about it all the time, and I just started to feel sorry for him." Because these victims do not perceive their mothers as allies, they remain dependent on their fathers for the parenting they need. They feel as though they have no other choice but to comply with their abusers if they don't want to lose the little love they are getting. Although the incestuous relationship is outwardly sexual, its meaning for these youngsters is deeply emotional. They come to accept their fathers' sexual advances as an expression of parental love.

Such children are powerless and needy within their families and have few, if any, options available outside their homes. What results, as many feminists have pointed out, is that many young female victims learn at an early age to subordinate their needs to the needs of others more powerful than they. And those "powerful others" nearly always are the men whom adult women serve as wives and sweethearts. Only to a greater degree than non-abused women do female incest victims accept responsibility for fulfilling the psychological, emotional and sexual needs of the men in their lives at the expense of their own well-being.

Evelyn

"I've spent so much time in my life thinking about this, talking with different people about it, and so much time being angry at my father, that I'm tired of it. I have spent my whole life trying to protect my parents from this horrible thing, this secret. As though they weren't participants in what happened.

"When I was seventeen I had my first consenting sexual relationship with a man and suddenly was flooded with memories which had been repressed about sexual behavior between my father and me. It was really overwhelming, and I was unable to remember what had been buried for more than five years. I became very depressed and began a pattern that continued for many, many years, trying to seek help for this problem—help I never adequately received.

"After trying many different kinds of ways to unlock other memories that are still unavailable to me, all I can

the children

recall is one time with my father when he was sexual with
me and one much more vague time with both my parents.
*Most of my childhood is blocked from memory, and I can
remember only isolated schools and experiences and I can
only guess at them. I've been guessing for most of my life
since I was seventeen. I can only guess that other sexual things did occur and I'm blocking them, or the power
of the times I do remember was so great that I had to close
everything off.*

"*I do remember when I was somewhere around eleven or
twelve—because I remember what I looked like and it was
pre-puberty—being awakened by my father's sexual advances. I had been asleep and woke up to find my father
being sexual with me. I recall being in a state of terror, not
quite knowing what was going on as I lay there for a few
minutes and allowed him to touch me. I remember the terror I felt and the confused feeling of being turned on. I
think I said no to him, but I've spent many years trying to
be sure of that.*

"*Even now, the memory has an unreal feeling to it, and
maybe that's because it's so isolated. There's very little else
surrounding it that I can recall. I think that's because I
haven't worked through much of it, and still, when I think
about this isolated instance, it feels so profoundly, deeply
wrong that it's just very hard to integrate.*

"*In addition to the sexual contact with my father, I have
other memories, easier to deal with, of his beatings, just a
vague sense of him being physically abusive to me as a
child. I remember a few times he beat me for reasons that,
because I was so young, were not apparent to me. But as I
got older and more psychologically sophisticated, at least
one of the beatings that I remember was that of sexualized
rage. He had awakened me in the middle of the night to
tell me that he didn't want me to sleep on my side. When I
protested that I was perfectly comfortable on my side, he
told me it was unhealthy and insisted that I sleep either on*

my back or on my stomach. I guess I said something sarcastic, and he told me that if I didn't turn over he was going to hurt me. And he proceeded to do just that.

"And I was confused. Besides the fact that it hurt and I was petrified, I was very confused about what precipitated that response from him. As I said, recently I could understand his behavior as sexual, but he was too threatened by his own feelings of sexuality and transposed them into a brutal form.

"Except for those few memories, it's all pretty vague. Mostly a feeling of growing up in an environment that was unsafe. Both my mother and father were violent people who had no control over their impulses. My mother used to beat me, my father used to beat me, they used to throw things at each other and fight, and the milieu in the house was such that I never felt my body was safe from violation. So that in my childhood, of all the feelings that were not tolerated, the one that was least tolerated was anger. Because I knew that if I wanted to express anger, I would really get hurt.

"So that I learned very young that if I were to survive whole in this family I could not be angry. So I certainly couldn't be angry at my father's sexual advances because that would surely have caused me to be dead—at least in my child mind. Likewise, all strong emotions were not allowed.

"I remember being about four years old and standing in front of the house, just before I was going to go in from playing, and I decided that the only way I was going to make it with my crazy parents was to shut myself off. I don't know if I thought about it in those terms, but I felt they were just too crazy, just too sick, just too unable to relate to me in a helpful manner. So I had to preserve myself by locking it up.

"When you talk about incest, it's difficult to separate out the consequences of it on your psychological development

and the general consequences of being raised by two people who were not grown-up. I think the 'not grown-up' part probably is true of most fathers who sexually abuse their daughters.

"I can't believe incest is an isolated type of behavior that occurs because somebody occasionally loses part of their control. So my own confusion about separating out the sexual behavior from all other behavior on the part of my father and my mother probably is normal for this sort of situation. It was a multi-problem family I came from, and the sexual acting out was just one of the symptoms of the problem. This affects me very much today as I struggle to undo the depression that has become habituated as a way of life for me. I've attached a lot of significance to the incest, in a way to protect myself, to keep me from dealing with the more profound violation, the violation that came from being emotionally neglected. Even now, what I do recall about my father is that even though I was in a state of terror, it was also in a way very positive, since my father's sexual advances toward me were the only recalled demonstrated love that was expressed to me in my childhood.

"Sex took on an overdetermined meaning for me. But in a real way, this was the only way my father had to express any feelings to me. Now that I'm thirty-one and it's been many years since my father touched me, things, incidents, remembrances keep surfacing that indicate to me the significant number of things that I have repressed.

"I try to remember whether there were any further sexual abuses by my father. I also have a very vague memory of being in bed with both my parents, in which my mother was laughing sort of strangely as she was biting my ass. That was a very sexualized experience, too. Although the memory's dim, it seems to add credence to my feeling of her not being able to protect me. Whatever she may have done to perpetuate sexual acting out is something else again, but what's clear is that she was not available to me

as a source of protection from my father, so that I have spent most of my whole life trying to unravel the mystery of my past.

"In recent years, I can remember that my parents were good people, good in a way that people in the milieu in which I was raised were generally not. My parents cared more for human values than for material ones, which made me, even when I was a child, aware that there was something special about them. But that specialness caused us to be even further isolated from the community and the family and the neighborhood. My mother would much prefer feeding a neighbor than buying a new dress. There was always that sense of her being different.

"My father was bright. I remember feeling good about that because my mother wasn't especially bright, and by bright I mean educated, actually. My father's involvement with the seedy part of life was a constant source of embarrassment for me. He was a gambler, and he sold pornography and was always involved with characters that were just not part of my larger family structure. My father was just not like the rest of my aunts and uncles, whether they were businessmen or teachers. They didn't sell pornography. They didn't gamble. Or at least it just wasn't clear whether they did or not. But I was more than embarrassed about my father; I was confused. He didn't make any sense to me. I couldn't fit him into any neat little categories.

"And my mother, too. She was different. If she didn't like something a neighbor said, she'd tell her in no uncertain terms, and she didn't play any of the social games that all the people around me, even at a young age, were playing.

"Mostly I remember feeling embarrassed, as I said, confused, very, very sad. I felt that my parents were constantly being rejected by the world for who they were. That used to make me very angry as a kid. I was always feeling angry at my relatives for rejecting my parents because they were more poor, or different, or just didn't count in the world, hadn't accomplished, hadn't achieved. But even then, I knew I couldn't act angry. It was very sad to see them rejected by a world that couldn't understand that it was okay to be a little different, not to buy a house in the suburbs, all those convenient things.

"My father has always pretty much worked. Except at one point during my childhood—I guess it was the heyday of his gambling—he was out of work for long periods of time. And then there were times during his working when he gambled so much that the paycheck wasn't totally secure. He's always been a civil servant and a white-collar worker. My mother never worked, except in the home. She worked very hard. It's sad for me to remember them, because my parents have always been people for whom life has been very difficult and who had very little support for themselves. As they got older they were able to maneuver a little better, and their lives are a little easier now.

"One of the most driving aspects of my quest for myself, or search to resolve all my conflicts in relation to the incest, is the hope that as I resolve this in relation to my parents, that I then will be able to make the last few years of their lives more pleasant for them. I have always felt sad about the fact that as I got older and more able to distance myself and my needs from them, I saw them as very sad people who have never had and will never be able to have any degree of satisfaction. I hope to be able to give them something more than I have. Not that it's my responsibility to take care of them . . . .

"As I got older, my impression of my parents changed. The most significant difference was the lessening of the shame. It no longer mattered or matters to me what the world thinks of me in relation to who my parents are. Because that was the nature of the shame when I was a child.

"I remember when my mother would go out into the real world. She wasn't the kind of person who was like everybody

*else, so that if we went into a restaurant, she'd start talking
to strangers or to the waiter. What I used to think was that
she was just very loose about her boundaries. As I got older
I began to see that she is very beautiful in that she really
doesn't give a shit. She really doesn't care what people
think of her, and I have much more respect for her now
than I ever did as a child. I feel very lucky. I feel that I'm
the only member of my nuclear family who has had a
chance at a fuller life. I don't know why that is, but it's
true. Because I was born with more endowments than
my parents or my brother, I have felt for much of my
life, and feel more strongly now, that I have a responsibility to share the fruits of those endowments with the
world—and, more specifically, with my family. And
somehow if I can break the chain, the cycle, that has
trapped my parents and my brother, somehow if I'm lucky
enough to break it down, then I want to help them.*

*"Several years ago I braved my father enough to ask him
why he beat me, and he denied it. He denied any manner
of gross abuse, and so I decided that if he was going to
deny that, I wouldn't ask him anything else. But I started
to have dreams in the past few years, just sort of impres-
sions that as a small child I had been sick. I asked my
mother if I had been sickly as a child, and when I asked
her, a sort of fog came over her eyes, which I noticed,
and then quickly she said, 'No, nothing was wrong.'*

*"I have never discussed it with my brother, with whom
I have a fairly close relationship. I never did because I
have always felt that my brother had had such a hard life
in relation to my family that I didn't want to burden him
with anything that would make it more painful than it
already is to deal with my parents. So even to this day
I'm protecting, even my brother. He developed patterns
very much like mine. Even though he's a college graduate
and lives a contemporary lifestyle, he lives with blinders
on. He just doesn't feel. He works very hard, comes home*

*after working six days, seven hours a day, and watches TV.
That's his life. He's married now, has a child, and he seems
to be repeating with his wife and child a lot of the same
trips he went through. Every time I reach out to help him,
to make him more aware of his choices, I'm met with a
wall. For whatever reason, I was born a little different
from my parents and my brother, so I could see things
more clearly than they seemed to see things.*

*"Even when I was little I had golden aspirations and
dreams and had a sense that there was light at the end
of this dark, dark tunnel. So I felt that my life was more
in my hands and I had more choices available to me certainly than my parents and my brother. I think the protectiveness arose from the sense that I had some control
over my life and they didn't. They experienced very little
self-control in relation to how they raised me. They beat
the shit out of me and they sexually abused me and my
father gambled and I mean it was crazy. They had no
control. It was like they were the children and I was the
parent. I was the peacemaker, and I was the one who
attempted to arbitrate between my parents when they
were fighting.*

*"I don't have as much of a handle on my efforts to pro-
tect myself as I do on my efforts for my brother, except
for the time when I was four and I remember just deciding
to hide inside myself. That's the ultimate self-protection,
a self-protection I still feel. The very ego defenses that
frustrate me in my existence now are the same qualities
that enabled me to survive with my power intact. It's
very ironic.*

*"I wouldn't be surprised, actually, if there were sexual or
sexualized interaction between my brother and me. As I've
said, I have very few memories left; but he and I shared a
bedroom until I was eighteen, and that certainly suggests
something, although I have no memories except of our
loving each other.*

conspiracy of silence

"I was four years older than my brother. I remember when I was about seven, I found a paper bag in the closet filled with pornographic photographs. I was old enough to know what they were, and I was horrified and titillated and intrigued. But some of them were pretty gross. I was sitting on the floor looking at them, just like agape, and my little brother came in. And in this bag were key rings with pornographic pictures on them, like cheesecake. My brother grabbed them and thought they were cute and ran outside to show his friends. But then my mother came in and found me with the pictures. I told her my brother had taken some outside, and she went running to get them back. And I remember thinking at that time that my brother was just too innocent and he didn't know what was wrong and dirty. He didn't know he had to protect the family from other people knowing.

"My mother was aware of the pornography, the gambling. There was lots of talk, too, about other women. My mother used to always tell me how terrible my father was. I was her confidant, so I became aware at an early age of my father's alleged sexual exploits with other women, the gambling, the lack of care for the family. And I shared my mother's fears when I was young that when he was out gambling that he might not come back, that we would lose him to some slut around the corner.

"And part of it that's important in relation to all this is my parents' verbalized attitudes toward sex. Though there was little communication within the family, what little there was, was such that led me to believe that my parents thought sex was dirty.

"That was important because my father thought sex was bad and wrong. I would get that from comments he would make about so-and-so next door who was not a virgin and she wasn't married. You know, I just remembered my father used to sing a song that he thought was real cute. The line I remember was 'All women stink.' Not only was

sex dirty, but from my father's point of view women stunk.
And they were the ones that were the wrongdoers. I just
couldn't understand the discrepancy somehow, that he and
my mother could speak so badly about something they
did. It just didn't make any sense.

"I think I have spent so much of my life seeing how they
have suffered in their lives that I have just not permitted
myself to feel the rage that's in me for having been abused.

"Much of the anger I carry around inside me about my
parents is directed at the world because I cannot understand. Somewhere deep inside me I'm furious that the
world would have let my father and my mother betray me.
There's a real anger at the unfairness that people I saw
every day, who heard what went on through the windows,
didn't try to help. And because it was never vented out,
it's still with me. But it's not just rage, though. It's sadness.
I just haven't been able to say, 'Well, that's the way life is.
People suffer.' There's this sad place inside that says, 'It
didn't have to be that way.'

"It was so hard when I was a kid, not being able to ask
for help, not being able to get it from a world that just
didn't care. But I feel a real sense of responsibility to other
people now who have suffered the kind of pain and loss
that I have. Because I know what it feels like. It's sort of
like a deal that I made. Okay, God, get me through this
and I'll be good. You know? And I do feel like I have to
help people. Because if I don't, maybe I'll kill them. But
that pain is human pain. What made my parents do what
they did to me? And what made the neighbors not listen?
And what made the teachers not answer? Were all the people running from that pain?

"I know that I explain and rationalize and defend because
there have been so few people, when I was young, when I
was growing up, or even now, that have been able to give
me some simple human comfort, kindness or help. Sometimes when I'm quiet or if I'm meditating, there surfaces

the sound of a scream. The feeling of the scream is one of horror of all the stuff that's locked up inside me that I'm so driven to unlock.

"I participate now, somewhat marginally, in a therapy group for incest victims, and I watch myself and my response to the other women's stories. I hear myself think a lot, 'How horrible!' or 'How could you have let that happen?' and I understand that the response I have to others is the internal response I have to my own childhood, my own experience that's much less available to me.

"My hunch is that any person who has been violated by a parent must have a response of horror, because somehow if you can't be protected in so basic a way by your parents, then some basic need is betrayed. Even as a young child I understood that I had to protect and help them because they were so clearly unable to put controls on their own behavior. But there were no outlets or comfort for me.

"I feel sometimes that I've grown up to be poison. If I let my power out, my meanness out, I will contaminate other people. That directly relates to the feeling of being this bad little girl who didn't use her power correctly to stop her father from assaulting her.

"Somehow I felt that I was responsible for my father's life. That it was me who caused his migraines and his ulcer. In a sense, it's not too far from true. Because if I had not been who I was, he might not have been tempted to lose control and suffered the consequent guilt I presumed he suffered through these migraines and ulcers, which he did not have prior to his sexual acting out. It's a tricky issue, my child's notion of power and responsibility. Sure, I was just a little kid, but I did feel I had some responsibility for what happened.

"My father reinforced my feelings as a child that I had no power to stave off his assault. But he also reinforced the notion that I had a lot of power, because if I hadn't had a

the children

lot of power, I wouldn't have seduced this grown man into sexually acting out. And somehow the experience with him exaggerated my child's sense of omnipotence. So from that time on, I grew up with a very distorted imbalance between feeling I had no power and feeling I had tremendous power.

"But when I try as an adult woman to let some of that power, vitality, strength out, it gets misinterpreted by the world—the world of men. I am called angry, hostile, overbearing, etc. I remember being in a group in New York City where you had to learn to deal with a lot of things on a street level. I remember learning at a young age that if you walk through the streets smiling and feeling happy, you had better be prepared for a sexual come-on from guys that see you. So you learn how to veil your eyes and convey the message that you're not interested. On a practical level, you learn how to deceive and to inhibit your feelings. On a larger level, I have learned that if I let myself be, I will not be understood. And that hurts in a very deep place. People tend to get threatened by their own unresolved stuff, and the feedback I get is, 'You come on like a bulldozer.' Somehow it's too much power. I see this as being related to issues of sexism, of my being a woman and of my options for expressing my power being culturally limited. Somehow, for women to express their power is alright only if that power is used in the service and helping of men.

"I hold it all in now, because for me to let out my power would also mean to let out the anger, the hurt, the memories of assault, and the fear of letting all that out . . . means that I would die."

THE AGGRESSORS

◆◆◆◆◆◆◆◆◆◆◆◆

Hal

In a visitors' room at the prison, he spoke softly into the phone, without lifting his head to look directly at me through the glass partition. He was pale, ordinary look-ing, not at all the slavering image many of us carry in our minds of a child-raper. He repeatedly wiped his hands on his prison uniform as he talked and chain-smoked nervously.

I had come to see Hal with a list of questions I hoped I would be able to ask him, but it became clear during our first visit that there would be no need for me to refer to it. Hal spoke compulsively about his experiences, without any prompting on my part.

"Hard as it is to talk about it," Hal told me, "I'm almost glad of the chance. Nobody comes to see me anymore now, and the other prisoners don't want anything to do with me. They treat me like I'm the lowest of the low. All I do is spend time going over and over it in my mind to figure it out."

Hal is forty-five and has been in prison for the past three years. He was tried and convicted of having sexually

the aggressors

assaulted his eldest daughter and was sentenced to five years by the horrified judge who heard the case.

"You should have seen how they all looked at me during the trial. Like I wasn't even human. I was so ashamed and pleaded for another chance to keep the family together, but they all turned their backs on me. Just wanted me out of their sight. That's exactly what my wife said—'Get him out of my sight!' My daughter was crying all the time she was on the witness stand, and it was so hard on her. She had to keep going over and over the same things, answering all their questions, and I felt so terrible that they put her through that after everything that I had put her through.

"When I heard the clanking of the door slamming behind me that first day, I came the closest I ever had to breaking down. It was inconceivable that I would end up in a prison cell. I sit here and go over and over it in my mind. Try to follow my life from the beginning to figure it out. I have nothing but time now, so I spend it thinking and figuring.

"Figuring is one of my big words. I'm an accountant, or at least I used to be. I was the first college graduate in my family, and it was a really high point in my life. In fact, it was the highest point. My father and I were never very close; he always felt I was ashamed of him. He's an electrician and always wanted me to follow in his footsteps. When I wanted to go on to college, he felt that meant I didn't think his life was good enough for me and my choice was a putdown of him. It wasn't, but my mother was always encouraging me to do better. I suppose in many ways I was her favorite and the one she thought would fulfill a lot of the dreams that had never worked out in her own life.

"The whole time I was in college, I never got a letter from my father. When I would come home on vacations and during the summer recess, he remained very distant and cold to me. My mother was supportive and encouraging and would always tell me not to pay attention to

my dad. She would say that he was just jealous of my chance for a different kind of life.

"After I graduated and married Ronnie, I had high hopes for our life together. Somewhere in me I wanted to prove to my father—I don't know exactly what—but there was a part of me that was a little kid wanting his approval. Things went along pretty well for a long time. We had three children, made a deposit on a little house, bought a camper for family holidays—you know, all the trappings of the good life.

"But then it all started somehow to slip away from me. It was so gradual at first that I didn't really notice what was happening. I guess I started to drink more. Not a lot. Just more than one or two, and nearly every day. That's a lot of alcohol for someone with my constitution.

"By the time ten years had gone by, I had tried to take the exam for C.P.A. every year and could never pass the last part, and it became one of my biggest disappointments. And every year I kept getting older, and a new crop of young men straight out of college would enter the company and I would be pushed aside for them. Guys in the firm for just a few years were making more money than I was.

"Ronnie was real disappointed in me, too. She never actually came out and said so, but I could tell. It was hard on her, the money being so tight all the time. She tried hard to manage things, but it was hard for her. And after a while she started to look and talk differently. Like I was a failure.

"My parents started acting like I was a dreamer who couldn't ever make things happen for his family the way he should. Our family is not one that's given to too much conversation about our feelings. We never have been. But you can just tell how people are feeling about you. Especially when that's how you're feeling about yourself.

"I guess this sounds like a whole lot of excuses and apologies. I don't mean for it to sound like that. I know what

the aggressors

*happened was my fault, although it took me a long time to
really make myself believe that. I blamed everybody else—
my mother for pushing me too hard, my father for not
believing in me, my wife for drawing away and getting cold
and distant. There were as many excuses as there were people in my life. I was sure bitter for a long time. Especially
when I remembered the dreams Ronnie and I had about
how our lives were going to be. I was going to give my kids
everything. It turned out that I gave them everything, all
right—a father who had sex with his daughter and lands
up in jail.*

*"I spent a long time trying to make believe it wasn't hap-
pening. Each time I would go into my room and swear it
would never happen again. But it was like a compulsion.
Patricia, that's my daughter, loved me so much. She never
looked at me like all the others. She would always tell me
that next year I would pass the test, get the promotion,
things would get better. She was always so encouraging.
I loved her so much and wanted to kill myself when I had
sex with her that first time. She let me, but I was the adult;
I knew it was wrong. I just didn't want to let myself know
what I was doing.*

*"By the time it started, Ronnie and I were hardly talk-
ing anymore. It was just get up, go to work, come home,
have dinner, watch TV, go to bed. Get up, go to work and
on and on like that. Every day was just like the day before.
Even on the weekends Ronnie kept out of my way. When
I would suggest we take out the camper and go someplace
for the weekend, she would always find some excuse to
say no.*

*"The boys, they are the youngest, would always be busy
with their friends, and it was always hard for me to spend
time with them. I suppose I had such an awkward relationship with my own father, I just didn't know how to be
really comfortable around them.*

"Patricia would always want to be with me. We were like

63

*best friends she always would say. In many ways she re-
minded me of when I was little and used to spend all my
time with my mother and when I was a young man and
Ronnie and I were first married. I'm not sure about all
that, and it gets confused in my mind. I'm not a psychiatrist and don't know how to figure that stuff out, but I
know it all fits together somehow.*

*"I don't know if I was trying to punish Ronnie for being
so cold to me, or my mother for taking away the support
and encouragement she gave me when I was younger, or I
was trying to recapture my youth or what. I can't figure it
out, just why. But I would never do it again, if they would
just give me another chance to be together with my family.
That's all I ever wanted. Just another chance."*

Hal was only one of the men with whom I spoke who presented a stark contradiction to the image many of us have
of incestuous aggressors. He was not illiterate, violent or
chronically alcoholic. There are some aggressors who fit
that description, but not many.

Instead, most male aggressors are uncomfortably familiar.
They are familiar in having been taught and in believing
that their lives should parallel societal definitions of appropriate masculine and sexual behavior. Familiar in that they
are trapped into believing that they will enter and pass
through their middle years in a constant state of sexual
virility. Familiar in feeling themselves solely responsible
for the care of their families. Familiar in their anxiety
about the onset of middle age and its diminution of the
dreams and expectations they once had. Familiar in not
knowing how to ask for what they need and talk about
what they feel and in being unable to care for themselves,
their wives and children in an expressive and nurturing way.

the aggressors

Familiar in their needs for affirmation and acceptance while being unable to reach out for them.

It is not these men who are monstrous; rather, it is the society that has defined them and taught them to define themselves as a consequence of their gender. When all else in their lives fails, they have been led to believe that the exercise of the power of their genitals will assure them of their ultimate competence and power. They are no more or less than any of us who believe that conflict can be resolved through sexual activity. The difference is that these men choose their own children as the sexual objects through whom they attempt to relieve feelings of uncertainty about their manhood.

Much of the isolation and punishment of the aggressor in intrafamilial sexual abuse is a result of society's insistence on denying any similarity between these men and the rest of us. We reserve our worst fury for those who violate the minds and bodies of the children whose lives, development and futures are entrusted to their care. We study them, we analyze them and we punish them, and still we fail to understand that male incestuous aggressors are, in all too many ways, the products of our society's beliefs about maleness.

The roots of incestuous assault are to be found in feelings of anger, hostility, insecurity, frustration and isolation harbored by aggressors. Furthermore, there are two personality traits which consistently characterize those who sexually abuse their children and which separate them from other men who may experience similar feelings of sexual stimulation with their children but do not act upon them: "One problem is a lack of impulse control, either sexual or emotional. This may be the result of transient stress or may be characteristic of the individual. The second problem is a confusion of roles. The child is regarded at times as something other than a child, or as a surrogate for someone else."[1] Dr. Roland Summit and Joann Kryso have identified these two common personality traits as a result of eleven years of community psychiatric consultation.

The concept we have of abusive parents frequently calls to mind images of battering, physically dangerous men; however, sexual assault is a much more subtle form of abuse. It is the abuse of trust—the trust the aggressor has assumed in having taken responsibility for the birth and care of a child, the responsibility he has taken upon himself to provide a safe and loving environment in which his son or daughter can develop into adulthood. He, and only he, has abused that trust. For no matter what the other family problems might be, the aggressor alone must assume the full responsibility for having chosen to eroticize his relationship with his child.

In trying to understand the many forms of incestuous assault, we can begin uncomfortably close to home. Although each family has its own ways of expressing love and nurturing sexual closeness, many people find the line growing blurred. One father, who for years had bathed his children while his wife prepared the family dinner, found himself compulsively washing his son's genitals until he ejaculated. Another man, at the time his daughter entered adolescence, began stationing himself in the hallway outside her bedroom door so that he could observe her unnoticed as she dressed and undressed. A third father urged his ten-year-old daughter to sleep in bed with him "just to snuggle and be close" when she had nightmares, then fondled her, explaining that he was trying to help her relax.

One young woman, whose father was "only" an exhibitionist and never touched her, still is besieged with nightmares and is unable to have satisfying sexual relationships with men her own age. "Can you imagine," she asked, "the terror of never knowing, when I would be sitting at the table doing my homework, coming home from school or getting ready for church, when my father would tap me on the shoulder and I would turn to find him grinning nervously, his face all red, standing behind me with an erection? When I would see him like that, he would run back into his room. But I never knew when it would happen, and I still have awful nightmares that my father is going to touch me and I'll turn around and see him like that. And I haven't seen or talked to him in over twenty years!"

Although such men are not labeled by the criminal justice system as sexually abusive parents, their behavior can be as devastating to their children as that of those who instigate explicit sexual contact.

In nearly all the studies of adult male sexual offenders that have been done to date, well over half, and in some cases nearly three-quarters, of the men studied who are serving time in prison were found to have been sexually abused as young boys without any intervention. Therefore, just as rigid definitions of maleness are passed on from generation to generation, emotional, physical and sexual abuse are behaviors exhibited by men who most likely experienced such abuse in their own childhoods. For it is in our homes that we learn or do not learn to develop ways of being loving, sensual and sexual, and, sadly, what these men learned from their parents they learned too well.

However, incestuous aggressors not only learn to have inappropriate expectations of their children and of adult family members, they also come to teach their children the same developmentally damaging lessons that, without intervention, will continue to perpetuate themselves from generation to generation. The following story illustrates the way in which abusive patterns of behavior can be perpetuated within families.

Andrew

Andrew sexually abused his two stepchildren. After extensive therapy, he is clearer now as to why such behavior was doomed to repeat itself and somewhat awkwardly offers himself as a "horrible example."

"I was the middle of three boys, born when my parents were thirty-one and thirty-three years old. My father worked as a mechanic, and my mother supplemented the family income by working as a waitress.

"I remember my mother as being a very neurotic woman and my father as an absolutely passive man. When I was small, I can remember almost every single day my mother would find a reason to yell, scream and insult my father. She would always be putting him down, making him feel small and inadequate. I never remember him saying anything in his own defense or yelling back. What I do remember was that he was always tired. He worked hard and was constantly worn out. I never can recall him touching or hugging me. Certainly, he never kissed me. You just didn't kiss boys. It wasn't manly.

"He was a real disciplinarian, though. Hitting boys was somehow more alright than kissing them, and he gave me and my brothers uncountable whippings with his belt. There were welts on my backside and legs that were sometimes so bad that I couldn't even walk to school. The only reason that the beatings stopped, or at least became less frequent, was because one day the welts were noticed in gym class and the principal wrote a note home to my parents. I never saw what the note said, but I do remember the beatings pretty much stopped after that.

"My mother played a really strange role in my getting beaten. She would wait for my father to come home so she could tell him about the things I had done wrong during the day, but then when he would pull his belt off his pants and get ready to whip me, she would start to cry and plead with him not to hit me. I never understood what that was about. She had to know that when she told him I was bad that he would hit me, but she would cry and carry on so while he was doing it that it was confusing to me.

"When I started school, I took a job as a paper boy to make some money. One of the stops on my delivery route was a hardware store where the man would always buy a newspaper and then invite me into the back room and offer me a nickel or a dime more if I would put my mouth on his penis. I didn't understand what was happening, but he wasn't scary in any way, and I knew that I would get some money if I would just do what he wanted. So I did.

"When I was eight years old, my mother decided that she couldn't cope with her three sons any longer, and she shipped my brother and me, the two oldest, to foster homes. That's just how it felt—being shipped out.

"Every one of the foster homes I stayed in for the next two-and-a-half years until she took us back home were places where I was either emotionally, physically or sexually abused. There weren't any happy memories of any of them. Not that there were so many happy memories when I was at home. But at least it's your home. That makes a big difference in how a kid feels.

"At one of the homes there was a teenage boy who used to play a game he taught me called 'doctor.' That was when he would perform, or at least try to perform, anal intercourse on me. In the same home, my foster mother had an unmarried sister who would spend hours bathing me and rubbing my penis. That always confused me, because although I was old enough to know by then that what the son was doing was bad, it never seemed as though anybody felt that what the aunt was doing was bad, too. We would be in the bathroom for an hour sometimes, and although there was only one bathroom in the house, no one ever came in to interrupt when she and I were in there together.

"By that time I understood sex was bad, because whenever anybody touched my penis they told me never to tell anyone what they were doing because I would get in trouble.

conspiracy of silence

So of course I never told. But I did know that it was wrong and bad. Somehow.

"The other kinds of abuse I received besides the sexual exploitation were repeated beatings. In one home they used buggy whips; in another they used a rubber hose. I didn't understand why they used a hose until I was much older and understood that it wouldn't leave marks on my body.

"All of the homes I was in during that time were, or at least pretended to be, religious families. They were always praying and looking to God for guidance. I could never believe that God would have told them to treat a little kid like that, but just decided that God wasn't looking out for me even if He seemed to be taking care of them.

"When I was nearly eleven and finally went back home to live, I had an extremely painful experience while I was playing with two little girls my own age. We all decided that it would be fun to take off our clothes and look at each other and went directly to a shed that was nearby, and they showed me their vaginas while I displayed my penis. That was all there was to it. It was a willing and mutual thing. In fact, when I remember it, they were as anxious to see what I looked like as I was to see what they looked like.

"I don't know who told, or if anybody saw us go into or come out of the shed, but within one day the whole neighborhood knew about it. Not a single one of the neighborhood kids were allowed to play with me because I was branded as a 'bad' boy. I was taunted on my way to and from school every day. My father beat me, and I understood that I was extremely 'bad' and nobody liked me. Nobody would speak up for me even though there were three willing participants. It turned out to be only my fault.

"By the time I was about twelve I was so desperate to have someone love and care for me, I was ready to do whatever was necessary. There was a janitor at school who liked to play with young boys, and I let him have anal intercourse with me. He gave me money every time, but it was never really the money. He was nice to me.

"This relationship had been going on for a few months, when one of the older boys in my school approached me and said that if I would fellate him in front of the other boys that he would do it to me. Of course I said yes, hoping that perhaps they would become my friends. Instead, when I finished, the other boy reneged, and they all laughed at me and ran away, leaving me there with my pants down around my ankles.

"It was about that time that I started to drink. I would cut school and just start to drink in the morning. It was the best way to get me out of whatever I was feeling. I would drink until I wasn't feeling anything at all.

"After about a year, things were so bad at home and at school with my bad reputation that I just didn't want to have to face it anymore. So I ran away.

"I went from city to city during those early years, and of course I didn't have any skills, didn't know how to take care of myself on the streets of strange cities, so I started to prostitute myself to men. I wasn't expecting that any of the men would like me the way the janitor had when I was just a kid. I did what they wanted, they paid their money and that was all there was to it.

"Thinking back on it now, the sex was more animal than human, but I never felt that then. It was just the way it was. I was still drinking pretty heavily during that time, and the streets were getting harder and harder for me because I wasn't a new face anymore.

"When I was twenty-one, I got married. She wasn't the first woman I had been with, but one of the first. Her father was an alcoholic, and her mother had worked for years as a phone operator.

"As a matter of fact, my mother-in-law told me that she had taken the night job deliberately so that she wouldn't have to have sex with her husband. Sex was her idea of the most disgusting thing ever visited upon women. I remember wanting to tell her it wasn't so hot for men either, but I kept quiet. Later, my wife told me that her father had molested her when she was small. I didn't know that when we got married. She just wanted to get out of the house; I could have been anybody. And I needed so much for somebody to love me and someplace to belong that I married her.

"Our sex life was rotten, and I continued to drink pretty heavily. The marriage went from bad to worse—losing jobs, getting fired, police looking for me, creditors looking for me, bad checks. And I resolved all the problems the only way I knew how. I ran. And I kept on running.

"In _____ I met a woman who was probably the most exciting sexual partner I had ever had. She loved me, she appreciated me, and I felt that finally I had found a haven and the desperate need I had to be part of a family would finally be fulfilled. She had been married before and had two children—a boy, six, and a daughter, eight. She was a pretty heavy drinker, too, and we would get drunk a lot.

"Almost from the very beginning I would fondle and molest both the children when we were alone together. It became a compulsion for me, a way of life. At every opportunity when I was alone with them or could arrange to be alone with them, I would touch their genitals and get them to touch me. After several months I began oral sex with them. They would bring me to orgasm and I would excite them. I never forced myself on them physically, but would take my time and get them turned on so that I could do what I wanted.

"The sexual exploitation went on for six years, until my stepdaughter reached fourteen. It was then that she let me know that my advances were no longer acceptable and if I continued she would tell her mother. I tried just one more time, but she was true to her word and told.

the aggressors

"My wife cried and swore and finally agreed not to call the police if I promised to get psychiatric help. I did go to one appointment, but never went back, and resumed business as usual. This time just with the twelve-year-old son.

"I knew if my wife ever found out she would leave me and take the children someplace where I would never see them again, but I just couldn't seem to stop what I was doing. So I ran. But I ran toward my future and my past, not away from them this time. I knew I had to change and stop what I was doing, so I went into therapy. I found a man who didn't look down on me because of what I had done and was really interested in helping me change.

"I can, after thousands of hours of hard work, understand that the chain that linked me to child-molesting started with my parents, and they probably got their attitudes and feelings from their parents and so on, back through all the years. That chain has finally broken."

Coupled with the self-perpetuating nature of most forms of abuse is the problem of the rigidly patriarchal values and world view held by so many male sexual aggressors, which is expressed in their attitudes and relationships within their homes and outside of them.

Most men have been socialized to believe that they should occupy positions of power in this society and expect to be loved and cared for by parents and wives as they go about making their mark on the world. But what if they fail to achieve the power and attention they expect will be theirs? When some men feel themselves to be powerless in the outside world, they become, while they are in their homes, utterly despotic. As our culture has taught them, their homes are indeed their castles, and they are the unchallenged rulers of that domain. Furthermore, if these men were raised in emotionally chaotic families that failed to provide them with warmth and love, they often will be unskilled when it comes to providing love and nurturing

for their own children. Because of their emotional imma-
turity, they may have unrealistic expectations of love
from their children rather than *for* their children. Men
in this situation, possessing little self-confidence and a
shaky sense of self-esteem, may begin to feel an increasing
rage at their lives, spouses and children. In the case of
incestuous aggressors, this rage escalates and becomes
directed at those around them who are less powerful—
their children.

In this situation, an incestuous aggressor is powerless in
the outside world and emotionally needy within himself.
He frequently is ingrown and reclusive and often is unable
or unwilling to participate in the community life around
him. Instead, it is within the bosom of his family that he
tries so desperately to satisfy his unfilled needs for power
and love. And, like many men, he chooses coercive sexual
activity as a means of trying to solve his emotional problems.

Warren

Warren is the third in a family of five children. His father,
a brutal and sadistic man, alternated between beating him
and his brothers for wrongs that were always unstated and
periods of religious zeal and prayer. The father saw himself as a God-fearing man, and it was only during his alcoholic bouts that he struck out at his sons in a raging and
silent fury.

Warren's mother was a passive and emotionally withdrawn
woman who was unable to temper her husband's excesses.
She remained both physically and emotionally in the background and provided no comfort and intervention during
her husband's rampages.

Warren and his older brother were responsible for most of
the parenting of their two younger siblings. There was no
open communication on the part of any of the family
members nor was it ever clear what the family rules were,

so that Warren remembers never knowing what behavior was permitted and what was not. His earliest sexual experience occurred at the age of eight, when he asked his sister to touch his genitals. She became frightened and ran to tell their father, who severely beat Warren.

Several months after the incident with his sister, Warren's father caught Warren masturbating and beat him again. Between slashes with a switch, Warren was told that such things would be permitted only when he became an adult. It was a sin for a child and fine for a grown man. Warren was never able to understand just when sex would be alright, but never felt he could ask.

Warren left home at sixteen, directly after his graduation from high school. His early sexual contacts were abrupt, awkward and unfeeling. He concentrated on developing an exterior of a competent, strong man to present to the world and was careful never to betray this image by permitting a moment of vulnerability or anxiety to surface. To anybody.

In his late teens Warren married a young woman similar to his mother in that she was a quiet, unworldly and inexperienced partner who would not threaten his carefully developed facade of strength and competence. Their sexual relationship was tense and unsatisfying, although neither of them ever discussed or even hinted at the problem. They simply did not have the language available to them to begin.

Warren felt it was important to be a good husband and provider, and he maintained that role during the first few years after their three children were born. By the time the children reached school age, however, he began feeling unimportant to his wife, who was spending more and more time with the kids and was becoming less accessible to him. He began to feel that his wife had "left" him, much as his mother had when he was small. Warren grew increasingly despondent, bitter and resentful about the course of his life, and by the time his oldest daughter was nine years old, he was indulging in longer periods of steady and morose drinking so that he could forget his troubles.

One such night, while his wife was sleeping, Warren went into his daughter's room and forced her to masturbate him, as he had tried to do with his sister years before. He said during his arraignment that the night with his daughter had been the most satisfying sexual experience he had ever had.

Warren is serving time on a state prison farm, which is society's way of punishing him for his behavior. But as much as he must take responsibility for whatever damage he has done to his child, have we truly gotten to the root of his problem?

It is too easy to look upon men such as Warren as degenerates and to see them as men with severe sexual pathology and intellectually inferior reasoning processes, men unable to distinguish right from wrong. Rigid control; alcoholism; abusive personality traits; unfeeling, alienated, jealous and despotic behavior; poor education; occupational dissatisfaction; unsatisfying marital relationships and immature sexual adjustment are scrutinized as causative factors in understanding the incestuous aggressor. Although many, and in some cases all, of these elements play a part in the personal psychodynamics of sexually abusive fathers, they cannot be isolated and observed apart from the complex human lives of which they are a part and thought to be understood. Such hastily arrived at "understanding" is presumptuous and arrogant.

Where and how do aggressors learn their behavior? Where and how do they learn how to be adults, parents, lovers and friends? Only within the context of understanding the damage a patriarchal society does to its young men can we understand their victimization as well. These men are victims, not only of their particular parents, school systems and economic circumstances, but of something more pervasive than the sum of all these things. They are victims of male-defined standards of appropriate behavior that leave little room for the acknowledgment of deeply felt and repressed needs for love, acceptance, nurturing and warmth; victims of not being permitted to feel and express the full range of human feelings and of not being taught to understand the strength in admitting weakness; victims of not being able to open their arms or hearts to others, never having experienced arms in which they were encircled and made to feel safe.

The following story points out the need for us all to re-examine some of our most closely held precepts about home and family, men and women, and the nature and price we pay for patriarchy.

Loren

Loren is the eldest of three children born to a small-town judge and his wife. Loren's father died when he was five, and his mother did not remarry until Loren was eleven. During that time Loren and his mother were very close, and he was clearly her favorite, the child on whom she showered all the love she had felt for his father. They slept together, watching television and telling stories, until she married a successful insurance broker. Loren pretended to be pleased and accepting of the new relationship so as not to jeopardize his singular place in his mother's affections.

Loren was a shy and quiet boy, had few friends and reserved all his love for his mother. After her second marriage, his mother had less and less time for him, however, and Loren spent much of his time lonely and alone.

Loren left home when he was drafted and returned immediately upon completion of his tour of duty. By this time his patterns of keeping his feelings to himself and trying to appear self-sufficient and invulnerable were firmly established, and to all outward appearances he was a careful, rather meticulous and taciturn young man.

77

Pierce College Library
Tacoma, WA 98498

conspiracy of silence

Within a year of his return, Loren married a woman from a neighboring community who was several years older than he, someone he felt was as strong and capable as his mother had been following the death of his father. He took a great deal of pride in his home, his wife's many accomplishments as a homemaker and his two daughters.

When he reached his thirties, Loren found it harder to maintain his carefully managed emotional balance and began having confusing and upsetting dreams. He remembered all the nights he had spent in his mother's bed feeling himself stroked and loved. He wanted to tell his wife, but felt she would be shocked and would think he was "sick." Instead of trying to tell her of his childhood experiences with his mother, he became more quiet and withdrawn from his family.

When he was thirty-seven, Loren had an accident at work and was unable to return to his job for several months. During that time his wife took a job as a waitress while Loren remained home, cooking, cleaning and caring for the children. He became increasingly tense, irritable and depressed during this period. He had recurring dreams in which he would reach out to his mother, who would remain just out of his grasp, or try to find his wife, who would be hiding, and he would wake up feeling angry and alone. The most upsetting part of the dreams, however, was that Loren would wake up feeling sexually excited and would hurriedly need to relieve himself. At the same time he would try to keep his mind as blank as possible to keep the upsetting dream images from intruding on his conscious state.

One night Loren awakened from one of his dreams and relieved himself, but this time it was inside the body of his eleven-year-old daughter. He simply went into her room, picked her up, took her into his bed and had intercourse with her. Silently and quickly.

The child told her mother what had happened, and Loren's

wife, without hesitation, reported him to the police. Loren was arrested and charged with incest before the morning was over.

During his trial, Loren said he didn't remember what he had done, but that he did not mind going to prison. He said he would never let himself be close to or trust anyone again and accepted his prison sentence without asking for favors because he did not want to owe anybody anything or need anybody to care about him.

The significant difference in Loren's life now that he is in jail is that the bars that have always surrounded him are now visible to other people. They had always been there, but no one had ever seen them before.

A family therapist recently told me that were I to meet many of her male clients, in therapy by court order for incest offenses, I would probably find them quite likeable. She does not find them significantly different from the general male population and describes them as glib, charming, quite manipulative, usually in control of most situations and dominating in social encounters.

Men who are reported as incestuous aggressors seldom have prior criminal records. They have little or no psychiatric history, are not necessarily excessive drinkers and appear to be of average intelligence and education. Their work histories are steady, and their marital histories primarily monogamous. Like most of the male population, they have few or no ways to identify, understand or ventilate their feelings in an ultimately coherent and cathartic manner. Like most men, too, they have had few, if any, examples of loving and tender males in their lives and therefore come to emulate faithfully the only model they do have. That model is one we all know well: the man who is strong, sexually virile and competitive with other men in the outside world, and who is powerful in his home, boss with his wife and authoritarian with his children. However,

conspiracy of silence

it is the case with many aggressors that when this socially prescribed model of behavior became inaccessible to them, with all other definitions of maleness rendered unacceptable by our culture, they turned to what they had been conditioned to believe is the final source of their strength: their genitals, which became their weapon, their catharsis, and their downfall.

Michael

Michael remembers his large, boisterous and enthusiastic family. His early years were warm and loving, and he spoke bitterly of how it all came to an abrupt end when he was eight years old.

One day Michael was playing with a neighborhood girl who was about his age when she suggested that they play doctor and look at each other. As they were both eagerly doing so, she further suggested that they "kiss bottoms." A third child came upon them and ran home to tell her mother what she had seen.

Michael and the girl hastily buttoned up their clothes and returned to their homes, not knowing what they would find but sensing that something was very wrong from the horrified expression on the face of the child who had discovered them and their innocent game.

Not only did Michael get his first and most painful beating that night, but thereafter he was branded as a boy that the mothers in the community could not trust around their daughters. He was increasingly ostracized, and his pre-adolescent years were painful and lonely ones for him.

Michael remembers feeling that he was "no good," and the only sexual contacts he had during high school were with girls who were called "tramps" and who were "bad" like him. Later, while he was in college, he met a woman who knew nothing of his ill-deserved reputation, and they married within a few months. Michael was happy and felt he had a chance for a new life with his shy, quiet and "good" wife. But that was not to be the case, as Michael recounted to me.

"I suppose looking back on it now, it started when she was about six. It wasn't anything I thought about to myself at the time, but that's when it started. Every time I'd get into a bum frame of mind, I'd just want somebody to talk to, and I felt I could never talk to my wife. She gets uncomfortable talking about feelings. And I needed somebody who thought I was terrific and could help me get over my depressions. My daughter placed me on the highest pedestal there was. Everything I did she thought was just about perfect. It started with just fondling her. She liked it, I could tell. She really enjoyed it when I tucked her in and rubbed her before she went to sleep. Sometimes she would touch me when I'd get hard, and she liked that, too. I loved all the kids, don't misunderstand me, but she was, well, she was just my special kid.

"That went on till she was about nine or ten—the fondling and sometimes we would kiss each other down there. Nobody was hurt by it, and it made us much closer. I did used to worry that my wife would find out about it, though. It wasn't what my daughter and I were doing, so much as knowing that if my wife found out about it she would probably take the kids and leave me. My theory about it now is that I never wanted to cheat on my wife. I wanted some real love, and I was getting that from my daughter. It wasn't something I had to pay for from some stranger. That was what was so special about it. It was so real.

"I would always tell her, anytime you want to stop what we're doing, you just tell me. She never did. Never came right out and said she didn't like it and that I should stop. So I just never did. And one thing led to the other, and by the time she was eleven we started to have sex. I was always careful not to hurt her; I was very gentle at first. Then it

just started to get out of hand. I would get more depressed
and worry about somebody finding out. And then I just
did the stupidest thing of all. Actually, the therapist says I
did it to get caught, and I wouldn't be surprised if he wasn't
right about that.

"My daughter and her girlfriend were playing in her room,
and I went in and just sat on the bed for a while watching
them. I asked my daughter if she told her friend what we
did together. She said no, and the other little kid looked
real interested; so I asked her if she wanted to see what we
did. One thing led to another, and before you knew it, she
had joined in. But then the girlfriend told her mother, and
that was the beginning of the end for me, just like a repeat
performance of when I had been eight.

"I feel really bad finding fault with my wife. Actually,
she was pretty good about most things—the house was always clean, the meals were always cooked nicely, she was
always very good at running the household. It was the sex
and the talking about things that used to really get to me.
I love sex, always have, ever since I started with the girls at
school who would let me. I could do it all the time. But
my wife would put me off, or if she would allow it, it
would be only so I could hurry up and get finished. I could
never really get into it and enjoy myself with her.

"There were lots of things she wouldn't ever do, specific
things that I really like. She would never touch me or kiss
me any place except on my lips. She would never experiment with different ways of doing it—just could never
seem to enjoy it. That was very frustrating for me. It was
like a big chasm between 'bad' girls, who enjoyed sex, and
'good' women, who didn't. The other part of it was that
she never wanted to talk except about everyday things. It
seemed as though that was all we ever talked about—the
car payments, the furniture needing re-upholstering, that
sort of thing. But never about anything that had to do
with feelings. She was like that with the kids, too. It got so

they just stopped trying to tell her things, same as me. She would make me feel so foolish sometimes for trying to tell her things, like I was acting like a little kid. It used to make me really mad.

"It was depressing, my job and all, and she just wouldn't give me any sympathy or encouragement at all. I really tried to get moved up the ladder but could never pull it off. The good jobs always seemed to go to the other guys. And I would come home feeling so low, and it would be a big fat zero. A man's home is supposed to be the place where he gets the love and attention and the caring he needs. Not in my home, I can tell you that.

"I'm not blaming her for what I did. Don't think that I am. But a man has his needs, too.

"You know, my theory about all this is about how men think they're supposed to be strong and in charge all the time. Religion teaches that, too. But, hell, nobody can be strong all the time. But when you're a man, it's a hell of a thing to admit that you feel weak or scared; so you don't. Or if you try, and it seems like your wife doesn't want to hear about it, you just stop telling her how you feel. I know it's not her fault, but it makes me mad when I think about it. It's like you're living in a damn box and can't get out. The job is lousy, the wife isn't interested and it's like there is nowhere to turn. I'm not trying to say that's a reason to molest your own kid, but, hell, those kinds of feelings have to come out some way or other. And with me it came out with my daughter."

Michael is not unique. For him, his daughter represented all the love, acceptance and nurturing he felt unable to get from his wife, and his sexual aggression was that of both the frustrated and insecure boy who had been caught and branded as bad and the angry and hostile adult man. In the incestuous relationship, his "daughter" was never really present; for who she was, what her needs might have been

and what damage the relationship might have done to
her were never even considered. She simply served as
a stand-in.

In the following story, told in the words of the victim
and her mother, the child was a different sort of stand-in.
For her father, she represented a chance to recapture the
young man within himself, courting his wife at a point in
his life before the onset of middle years, bitterness, divorce
and social alienation had taken their toll.

Claudia

"The best way I can describe what kind of father David
was, was when Nancy was fifteen. It was her very first
prom, and she had been excited for weeks about it. She
had been up in her room for hours, painting her nails and
fixing her hair. When she finally came down the stairs in
her long dress, smiling so nervously, David got up from the
sofa and waited for her at the bottom of the stairs. He
bowed and asked if he could have the first dance of the
evening. He was terribly courtly and elegant, and he put on
some music and spun her around the living room. By the
time they had finished, she was all flushed and looked even
lovelier than she had at the bottom of the stairs, because
she knew her father saw her as the most beautiful girl in
the world. And he always has, and she's always felt that.

"From the very first minute she was born, they have
always been close. David and I were divorced when Nancy
was nine, but he always spent every spare minute with her.
Neither of us ever remarried, although we both nearly did
once or twice. But I just don't like being married all that
much, and David just said he wasn't ready to make that
kind of commitment to anybody else. In fact, right after
the divorce, he took Nancy for a while, but it didn't work
out at all. He was gone all day at work, and there was never
anybody home when she got back from school. So she
came back home, but David was as attentive to her then as

he was when we were together. He always knew the names of all her teachers, went to all the school plays, things not too many fathers ever did. And it used to make Nancy so proud of him.

"I took the divorce pretty hard. He had been involved with a woman in his office, a much younger woman, and it hit me right in the stomach. I suppose, looking back through all that's happened to us, that I didn't behave in a very stable way during that time. I was angry and hurt and did a lot of things I regret now. But you just can't hold onto somebody once they want out.

"And Nancy felt loyal to both of us and was too young to understand what was going on. Actually, I never really tried to explain it to her because I thought she was much too young to have to hear things like that. David didn't really want the divorce, to hear him tell it now. He says that I made him leave and thinks that our separation was my fault. I certainly didn't want to stay married to a man who was having a relationship with some other woman. But he twists things around like that; he always did. I have finally learned not to feel guilty anymore about things that are not my responsibility. That night after Nancy left for the dance, David stayed around a while and had a few drinks and tried to make a pass at me. After all the years in between—like they hadn't happened. I insisted he leave at once, and he walked away with his tail between his legs like a whipped puppy.

"It was soon after that night that I found out he and Nancy were lovers. It wasn't play-acting. He literally seduced his own daughter. And to this day I wouldn't have known about it if he hadn't started acting jealous and protective toward her.

"Nancy started to act more and more unenthusiastic about going to her father's for the weekend. Before, she had always looked forward to being with him, but she started to change and spend a lot of time in her room and be very quiet around the house. By the time she finally told me, they had been having sex together for nearly a year. At first it was like a boyhood dream come true for David, but after a few months he started acting real bossy with her, wanting to know everything she did and everyone she saw during the week, when she wasn't with him. Finally she just broke down and confessed to me what had been going on. She said she felt like he had her in a prison and wouldn't let her out."

I met Claudia and Nancy at a meeting of a victim-run peer-counseling group in southern California. Claudia was eager to talk about her experiences, to ventilate them, in hopes of cleansing herself of her feelings of guilt and responsibility for not having known what had been happening in the changing relationship between her ex-husband and child.

Nancy, too, feels guilty and responsible. She feels guilty for having played "girlfriend" to her father's "boyfriend" and responsible for letting it happen. She cannot yet understand the vastly superior powers of seduction her father utilized as he frantically and sadly tried to relive his own youth and a relationship he remembered having had with a woman who used to look like her.

In cases such as this one, in which the incestuous father is relating to his daughter in an adolescent fashion, the "courtship" tends to follow a common course.

Nancy remembered: "While it was going on, during that whole year, I was not allowed to have any kind of life outside the house. No friends, especially no boyfriends, no parties, no dances, not even a Saturday afternoon football game. He made sure he called all the time during the week so he knew where I was every minute of the day and night. And God help me if I didn't have a good reason for not being at home right after school let out. He used to give me lots of presents, extra spending money, things like that. But at the same time he was giving me things, he would get real ugly and threaten me with all kinds of awful things if I stepped out of line."

In an abrupt shift of roles, Nancy's father had altered his behavior from being the young boy currying favor with his sweetheart to being an all-powerful father who had the "right" to protect and define the rights and lives of his children.

Upon reaching the midpoint in their lives, a period in which their marriages are most subject to change through death, separation, divorce, unmet career goals, sexual maladjustment and estrangement between themselves and their partners, many men find themselves feeling boxed in and angry. Most often, too, this is the period when a man's eldest daughter is reaching puberty and is especially attractive and vulnerable. The daughter is incapable of retaliation, while the father, who may have had little or no experience with considerate and loving sexuality in his childhood or present relationships, may see sex as a powerful vehicle through which he can regain his "lost" manhood and youth.

In some situations, as in the following case, an angry father who is feeling pushed aside and insignificant in his home may use his child as a way of punishing his wife.

Vincent

Vincent would not permit me to interview him in person but finally consented to talk with me in a series of lengthy telephone conversations. He is in therapy with his family now, and he acknowledged that what he had learned might be helpful to others still floundering in a maelstrom from which they cannot extricate themselves.

"Sex was a big part of it. For a long time I thought that was all there was to it, but I am beginning to learn otherwise.

"My wife and I are both Catholics, and she really had

drummed into her all the teachings about sex and marriage and children. I did, too, but when I was growing up at least there were girls with bad reputations you could fool around with and get some of the pressure off. I had been with a lot of prostitutes before we got married, but I stopped the very day we tied the knot. She was a virgin, we were in love and I was going to keep all my business in the house.

"But it didn't turn out as easy as that. From the very first, she didn't like sex. I tried every which way to please her, but she always cried before, during and after. Not out loud crying, but sniffling, always telling me it hurt and to hurry up and get off her because I was heavy. It was real frustrating. I could never get her to talk about it either. I would try to ask her what she wanted me to do—something I'm sure my father never thought to ask my mother, I can assure you of that—and she would get all embarrassed and try to change the subject.

"So the sex was just lousy, and I was finally reduced to masturbating. A grown man having to do that, like a little kid. It made me furious at her every time. Of course, divorce was out of the question, and actually it never even occurred to me to think about. Being raised a Catholic like I was, it was just never a possibility.

"I worked steady as a construction worker all the time we were married and brought all my money home. At least in the beginning. But after the kids were born and she never seemed to have time for me at all, I wasn't in such a big hurry to rush home. So I used to hang out with some of the guys at work, and I guess I got into the habit of taking a few too many. By the time I would get home, I didn't give a damn whether anybody paid attention to me or not because I was so worked up by then. There were sure plenty of women in the bar I could have gone with, women who would have been glad to have me. You don't know what I look like, but there have been plenty of women who look me up and down. Plenty.

the aggressors

"Our first kid was the wife's favorite. It seemed like she spent all her time sewing her dresses that she didn't even need, giving her more spending money than a kid her age should have had, helping her with her schoolwork. Time, I guess now, I felt she should have been spending with me. It got so I was so angry at both of them that I would just come home and slam around the house hollering at everybody in sight. Damn, I wasn't even a man in my own house! Just some clown who brought home the bacon.

"When I would get to drinking, by the time it started to wear off I would be mad and depressed, and it would seem like all I could do to feel better was to have sex. That was my pattern. And she sure had her pattern, too.

"The night it happened, I came home and wanted some attention. My wife gave me her old song and dance about being too tired, having a headache, all that same old tired stuff she had been pulling on me all along. So I just sat in the living room after everybody had gone to sleep and drank myself into some kind of stupor, because the next thing I remember I was having sex with my own kid. She was just twelve then, but real developed for her age. I didn't even know how I got into her room, like I blacked out or something.

"I wanted to kill myself right then and there but made her promise never to tell anyone what had happened because of the shame. I told her she'd be shamed, I'd be shamed and the whole family would be shamed. And that if she told, it would be on her account whatever happened.

"I tried to keep away from her after that time—I would even go out of the room when she came in—but it happened again a few months later. After that second time, it just kept happening more and more often. Every time I would drink and get to feeling angry and depressed, it would just happen. It's ironic because she was just the same as my wife. She'd lie there and cry the whole time.

"When she finally told her mother after I got too forceful

and made her bleed, I was secretly relieved. It was finally out of my hands to make it stop. It was as though my whole life was out of control, and I didn't know how to understand what was happening and put the brakes on."

Vincent, like many men who were raised in very traditional families, urgently needed to maintain the role of powerful patriarch in his home. Part of what a man expects in a traditional family situation is an adequate, if not totally satisfactory, sexual relationship with his wife. He may not know how to develop such a relationship, or even understand that such a relationship needs care and nurturing, but assumes instead that it will automatically be part of his conjugal "rights." If the sexual relationship deteriorates, or if his wife is awkward or uncomfortable with her own sexuality and he has no understanding of the ways in which her discomfort might be alleviated, he can, like Vincent, feel angry and unloved.

Vincent needed to bolster himself, however temporarily and at an incalculable cost, at the expense of his child. Although he has spent time in therapy unraveling his relationship with his wife, he must face the central fact that he, and only he, is responsible for the sexual abuse of his daughter.

Many therapists who have had experience working with incestuous aggressors find that this central admission of responsibility is the most difficult and demanding part of the work done in treatment. When incestuous abuse comes to light, most aggressors construct elaborate defenses, rationalizations and excuses in an attempt to absolve themselves of their guilt and to avoid accepting responsibility for what they have done.

Such rationalizations can take many forms. One young victim told me that her stepfather persisted in having oral sex with her until she reached orgasm. Then he would triumphantly announce, "See, I know you enjoy it just as

much as I do. You wouldn't come if you didn't like it."
This woman is only now beginning to trust her sexual feelings with her own husband. She explains, "I felt like not only was I being raped by my stepfather, but double-crossed by my own body. I hated it, every minute of it, but my body just betrayed me. It was as if it weren't even connected with what I was feeling at all."

Another aggressor, who abused his niece, insisted to his arresting officers that every time he came to visit his sister, the victim, then only ten years old, would behave in an explicitly seductive way toward him: "She was always wriggling around, shaking her butt right up at me. I knew what she wanted. Now she turns around and hollers rape. But I knew what signals she was giving me."

Some men contend that it was their job to teach their daughters the facts of life. One father tried to vindicate himself by explaining that his daughter was already sexually active and that he was just trying to keep her out of trouble. "I didn't want some young kid knocking her up," he explained to the court-appointed psychiatrist.

Whatever the rationale, in order to preserve their wavering self-image in the face of the community's condemnation of their acts and to ward off considerations of the consequences to their victims, aggressors often place the blame, guilt and responsibility outside themselves and their control. Thus a victim and her mother often have an additional burden to carry: they are accused and held responsible for a father's actions. In some cases the child is described by the aggressor as provocative, seductive and willing. In others the wife is blamed for being frigid, absent, threatening, rejecting, indifferent or hostile.

Men who turn to their children for the emotional nurturing they may never have received from their parents and the sexual fulfillment they may no longer be receiving from their wives are taking the most destructive option available to them. Conditioned to having their needs met by women, unable to articulate or provide for such needs themselves, they alter the relationships within the family by substituting their daughters for their wives. Locked into rigid societal roles, they cannot understand not being cared for, nurtured, respected and loved by a woman, for that is what women are "supposed" to do. They are to love their husbands, be sexually available on call, be good mothers, manage the household, alter their activities according to the wishes of their husbands and not be demanding or aggressive.

Many men are not comfortable in situations in which their wives are unavailable or unwilling to adhere to the traditional wife/mother role, or when family circumstances demand a redefinition of traditional responsibilities. In a recently published study, the authors speak directly to this central dynamic of male socialization: "Fathers who feel abandoned by their wives are not generally expected or taught to assume primary parenting responsibilities. We should not find it surprising, then, that fathers occasionally turn to their daughters for services (housework and sexual) that they formerly expected from their wives."[2]

This situation also is illustrated in the words of another professional: "In another case incest took place when the patient was unable to be gainfully employed and the wife, who had to support the family, had relegated the husband to the role of a babysitter."[3] In this case, not only was the wife seen as having usurped the husband's manly role of supporting the family, the very fact that she stepped into the role that was called for by changing family circumstances made her appear to be abandoning her prescribed duties. Furthermore, the role of babysitter, as we all are led to understand, is appropriate for a young girl and certainly not work for a grown man.

Perhaps the most insidious aspect of incestuous assault is that in the same way men have been societally permitted to be sexual predators, their daughters have been trained into the role of victim by virtue of their femaleness. However, there are exceptions. One astonished social worker described a situation to me in which quite the opposite was true. The father had sexually abused three of his four daughters in stepladder fashion. He instigated the sexual activity gradually when the children were quite small and led them slowly and carefully toward intercourse. As each daughter became old enough to leave home, he moved on to the next one. When he finally was brought before a family court, he was asked why he stopped with the third and next-to-youngest daughter and made no effort to continue his sexual activity with his youngest girl. The man shrugged and said, "I tried with her. But the first time I did, she just looked at me and said no. So there was no point in trying again. She just wouldn't."

Saying no takes an extraordinary amount of strength. It is a word that women are not comfortable saying to their men, children to their parents and these men to their damaging impulses.

THE MOTHERS

◆◆◆◆◆◆◆◆◆◆◆

Robert and Andrea

Robert grew up in a poor, traditional Italian family in the Italian ghetto of a large, northeastern city. Robert's mother was a strong, silent woman who had learned to tolerate her charming, boyish, life-of-the-party husband. His father was a marginal and inconsistent wage-earner, so his mother worked part-time to augment the family's income. Robert was prodded repeatedly by his mother to achieve the professional status and material stability his father had been unable to attain. His older brother became a doctor, and all his sisters married upwardly mobile men. Robert remained close to his mother emotionally and felt a great need to share all his triumphs with her. His feelings for his father were more detached and pitying, and he sees his father as "different" from him.

Andrea grew up in a culturally transitional household similar to that of her husband. Her mother had been married three times and assumed the role of matriarch in each relationship. Although her background was patrician,

the mothers

Andrea's mother vacillated between contentment with her traditional female role and an eager desire to experiment with alternative lifestyles. The black sheep of her conventional family, she was a source of confusion and ambivalence for Andrea during Andrea's childhood. Andrea's two older brothers chose a religious life, one as a monk and the other as a minister, and her younger sister is a housewife who has been in intensive therapy for years trying to make her "marriage work." Andrea was taught by her mother that she was the smart one and her sister the beautiful one.

Andrea and Robert met in college, and their courtship followed the traditional pattern. Robert acted as a strong, assertive male, and Andrea counterbalanced him by being passive, acquiescent and by following his lead. Being with a dominant male was a new experience for Andrea after the succession of men her mother had married, and she delighted in the emotional security it afforded her. The couple's courtship consisted of regularly scheduled weekend dates with only a minimum of experimental sexual play. Both of them agreed that sex belonged in the marriage bed and not before.

Robert and Andrea had a big wedding that was the high point in Andrea's life. Everything she had read and believed in the magazines of the 1950s played a part in the planning of the ceremony. Both partners remembered their brief honeymoon fondly, with the exception of disappointing sex. Robert went from the marriage bed into the service. Andrea faithfully waited for her husband's return, having decided their sex life undoubtedly would take time to become rewarding. She did not permit herself to feel let down about the sex Robert defined and instigated at what he considered to be appropriate intervals. As she explained, "It was in the dark. In bed. In silence." Andrea had no one with whom she could discuss "personal" matters, so she pushed such concerns aside, continued her schooling and gradually fixed up a home to be ready for Robert at the end of his tour of duty.

When Robert returned, Andrea immediately quit school so that he could begin a master's program in biochemistry. Both of them remembered this as being one of the happiest periods of their marriage. They felt they were working together toward a shared goal. Though their sex life continued to be as silent and abrupt as it had been since the beginning, it seemed the only area of Andrea's life that wasn't satisfying; so she simply continued to keep it to herself.

While Robert was concluding his master's, Andrea became pregnant. Instead of going right into a Ph.D. program as he had expected to do, Robert accepted a good job with a large corporation. The couple worked to convince each other that the Ph.D. could wait and everything would be just fine. They began to plan for their first child with eager anticipation. Unfortunately, Andrea contracted German measles during the early months of her pregnancy, and she was advised by her obstetrician to abort the fetus. Robert concurred with the diagnosis, but Andrea's Catholic upbringing along with her anxieties about the procedure led her to refuse and hope for the best.

The couple's child, a boy, was two years old before he finally was diagnosed as severely retarded. Once the child's brain damage became obvious, Andrea and Robert spent a tense and argument-filled year and a half wavering between institutionalizing their son and keeping him at home. The child took all of Andrea's time and attention, and she began to resent the apparent course of her life, feeling powerless to alter it. The factor that decided their son's hospitalization was the onset of Andrea's second pregnancy.

Although they seemingly agreed then to "put him away," Andrea felt both guilty and relieved at the decision while Robert submerged anger at what he then felt was his wife's avoidance of a mother's responsibility. Neither expressed his or her feelings to the other, and the couple developed a cautious shorthand form of communication chosen expressly not to touch on areas of possible tension or unresolved conflict between them.

After the birth of their second child, a girl, and the hospitalization of their son, Andrea had a minor flirtation with a neighbor. She fantasized it into an elaborate love affair, and the occasional moments when she saw this man in the drugstore or supermarket became the high points of her day. She imagined each casual exchange to be important and full of meaning, and she began to spend more and more time in the house thinking about her "love affair."

Six months passed, and the imagined affair became in Andrea's mind the most central and important part of her life. She confronted Robert with this distorted information in an angry and aggressive way. Demanding a separation, she told him that this man would listen to her when she talked about personal things, that their sex was spontaneous and passionate and that the man cared for her to the exclusion of her child. In short, she manufactured a man who was what Robert was not.

Robert agreed to a separation without argument. He was angry and hurt, but his pride would not allow him to seek a way to salvage the disintegrating relationship. During the three weeks of their separation, Andrea developed a conviction that she was being followed. Feeling paranoid and frightened, she called Robert and told him her anxieties about being alone with the baby and the guilt she was feeling for having broken up their family, then asked him to return. She also told him that she had been hearing voices and that she kept having dreams in which the face of their son looked at her accusingly. Robert came home at once and, without a word to Andrea, packed their daughter's things and took the child to his mother's house. The same day he began to take steps to have Andrea hospitalized.

conspiracy of silence

*Andrea was diagnosed as a schizophrenic and was hospital-
ized for a period of seven months. The day she was released,
Robert drove her to a large, totally unfamiliar house in an
upper-middle-class suburb. He had bought the house as a
"coming-home present" and explained that it was something to keep her "mind occupied and days full."*

*Within two months of her release, Andrea became preg-
nant again, and she made a herculean effort to accept her
female role. She worked incessantly to keep the house
clean, look after her small daughter and be the sort of wife
she had promised Robert she would be during their courtship. Feeling guilty and ashamed of her hospitalization, she
promised herself that she would live on the emotional
straight and narrow and not allow herself to imagine things
that were not true.*

*After the couple's second daughter was born, Andrea had
another breakdown—again on the anniversary of their son's
hospitalization. Her symptoms were more intense this
time, and she was utterly convinced that she was both a
prisoner of her husband and a "political prisoner like the
Statue of Liberty." She distrusted Robert and his efforts
to convince her that she was not a prisoner. He kept insisting that he loved her and would take care of her. All she
had to do was what every woman dreamed of doing: take
care of her lovely home, be a good mother to their two
beautiful daughters and stop thinking the world was any
different for her than it was for anybody else. "Stop being
childish," he repeatedly told her. "You're a grown woman,
and it's time you began to act like one."*

*Robert's speeches did not diminish Andrea's need to dis-
tance herself from her life. She was institutionalized again
for a year and a half, diagnosed as a paranoid schizophrenic.
Andrea was convinced that her husband didn't love her,
and the doctors were convinced she was out of touch with
reality.*

During Andrea's second hospitalization, Robert hired a

housekeeper to look after their home and children and saw to it that things ran as normally as they had when Andrea was home. He began having a series of meaningless affairs with secretaries from his office as a way to compensate for his wife's physical and emotional rejection of him. The secretaries with whom he slept never found fault with his lovemaking "technique," and he was very much in demand by the young women as a lover. Robert was careful not to get too involved with any of them, however, because he took his responsibilities as a father seriously. He had dinner with his two small daughters every night, read them stories at bedtime and spent nearly all weekend with them. He saw himself—and was seen by both his and Andrea's families—as a kind, much-put-upon man doing the best he could to sustain his home and family in the face of insurmountable odds.

During this time, Andrea felt the hospital was trying to teach her how to be the kind of woman that she was unable to be: "They were always after me to comb my hair, fix the hem on my dress, wear makeup. I caught on pretty fast that they saw those things as signs of progress, and I was never going to get out of there until I started to 'care for my appearance.' So I made believe, and it fooled them."

After her second discharge from treatment, Andrea decided to return to school and continue her interrupted studies. Robert and her hospital psychiatrist met and decided that she could continue her education as long as she stayed on a daily dosage of Thorazine to preclude any repetition of her "illness." Robert's anger began to surface more and more frequently in the relationship, however. He began to pick at Andrea for little things and complained constantly to his mother about what a failure he had chosen for a wife. Robert's mother sympathized with him and assured him she would be delighted to take the children should Andrea have another "breakdown."

During this period, Andrea was feeling under constant

conspiracy of silence

pressure from Robert, who, she said, "was always looking at me as though I was going to explode right in front of him. Just scatter into little pieces all over the room." There was little communication between husband and wife, except of the most mechanistic nature. Robert decided to keep the housekeeper who had cared for the children while Andrea was away.

Andrea returned to school, grateful to her husband for letting her go, and did quite well for a few months. However, one of her courses took her back into her childhood neighborhood during a research project, and the physical proximity to her earliest sources of inadequacy, coupled with the time of the year her son had been institutionalized, caused her anxieties to resurface. She told Robert she wanted to leave the marriage and be alone. "He was doing fine without me," she remembered. "The housekeeper took care of the girls. It was like he didn't even want me to be near them, like my illness would rub off or something. I didn't serve any function in that family, so I just decided I might as well leave and try to make some kind of life for myself away from all of them. Make a new start."

Robert would not let Andrea leave, however, and patiently explained to her that the Thorazine she was taking made her feel the way she did. He convinced her to put herself in his hands and everything would be fine. "I wanted so much to believe him," Andrea explained, "but I kept having doubts. Doubts that I could be a good mother, doubts that I was being a good wife. Robert was so patient and so forgiving with me. But every time I tried to remember that, I would get this awful red feeling of anger at him, and I wanted to have him evaporate into thin air and leave me alone with the girls. I just knew everything would be fine if I could just be alone with them."

A few months later, Andrea, Robert and the two girls were in their rumpus room preparing a Halloween jack-o'-lantern for the front porch. As one of the girls started to

the mothers

sing the nursery rhyme about "Peter, Peter, pumpkin-eater,"
Robert interrupted the child to turn to Andrea and tell her
that he "could do that" to her. "You couldn't keep me in
a pumpkin," Andrea remembered telling him with a nervous smile. "Yes, I could, if I cut you up into little pieces,"
Robert replied. By the following day, Andrea's increased
anxiety had convinced her that Robert would try to kill
her if she let down her guard for even a minute. Certain
that her husband wanted the girls for himself, that he was
tired of all the trouble she had caused all of them, Andrea
became increasingly suspicious, watchful and fearful.

Andrea's mother and mother-in-law added to her sense
of immediate danger. Both mothers made it clear to
her that they simply couldn't understand why as sweet
a girl as she, with such a good husband and two lovely
daughters and all their affluence, couldn't be happy.
Andrea continued to withdraw and to feel more and
more alone. Within two months, Robert decided to send
her back to the hospital.

Robert and the psychiatrist Andrea had been seeing had
developed a close relationship and met once a week for
golf. During those afternoons, the doctor shared information about his sessions with Andrea, and Robert was constantly up-to-date on his wife's "progress." The doctor felt
that since Andrea had not had a consistent and stable father
figure in her life, she was using him (the doctor) to fill that
void. The doctor encouraged the transference, feeling that
it was a healthy response and that Andrea's dependency
could then become the root from which she could develop
an acceptance of her life with Robert. The doctor assured
Robert that Andrea's "delusional" response to his "joke"
about the pumpkin affirmed a diagnosis of paranoid schiz-
ophrenia, since Andrea seemed utterly unable to tell the
difference between a joke and reality.

During her subsequent hospitalization, Andrea's delusional system became even more elaborate. She became

convinced the television and radio were telling her she was her husband's prisoner and that nothing she could do would set her free.

Robert began to withdraw from Andrea more and more and decided that once-a-month visits were sufficient. "Every time I went to see her it just made matters worse," he explained.

In the past two years Andrea has been in and out of the hospital six more times. She will not be released again until the experts are convinced she finally and fully "understands" that her fears of Robert are madness and "realizes" that she really wants nothing more out of life than to be a good wife to her husband and a good mother to her children.

Note: *Robert "allows" his eldest daughter to stay in "Mommy's bed" during the times Andrea is away. It is their "secret," and the daughter is not to tell Mommy when Mommy is home. Andrea has been taking fewer and fewer visitation privileges and is spending most of her time in the hospital. Her doctor's prognosis is the silent closing of a smooth steel door: "Recovery unlikely."*

Mother. Is she sick, or simply sick and tired? Who is this woman nearly all psychiatric literature defines as "colluding," the woman who permits the incestuous assault to happen, either consciously or unconsciously, the woman who is thought to be the invisible third partner in the sexual act between husband and child?

Mothers of incest victims are seen as cold, passive, withdrawn and dependent figures who are scrutinized, blamed and ultimately impaled on the sword of male-dominated analysis.

It seems clear that mothers who consciously or unconsciously avoid knowledge of the sexual aggression of their

the mothers

spouses in order to maintain a precarious sense of security in their lives, however ephemeral, pay the highest price a woman can pay: the offering up of her children.

I did not understand how mothers could remain blind to the sexual assaults inflicted upon their own flesh and blood, but after listening to many women whose sons and daughters had been sexually victimized by their fathers or stepfathers, some reasons became clearer to me.

Louise

Louise has been living with her three youngest children since her husband was arrested and her eldest daughter taken out of her home. She is seeing a therapist twice a week to try to understand how and why her life fell apart.

Louise spoke to me in a slow, hesitant manner. She paused often, searching for just the right words to express what she was feeling as we sat together for several hours.

"I know the doctor thought I should have been a better mother or a better wife. He didn't actually come right out and say that, but I could tell what he was thinking. He kept frowning and clearing his throat while I spoke.

"My home wasn't all that hot when I was growing up. There were too many kids, and my dad could barely make a living. The money never seemed to stretch far enough. He left when I was eleven. Since I was the eldest, I took care of the younger children because my mother couldn't seem to keep up with everything that had to be done. She changed after my dad left. She had to go on public assistance, which was real hard. I guess she had nobody to be angry at, except me. I know that was unfair, and it used to make me feel worthless. Nothing I could do would ever please her.

"When Frank came along, he was like no one I had ever known before. He was older and seemed so sophisticated.

103

conspiracy of silence

He said he cared about me. Nobody had ever said that to
me before he did. When he asked me to marry him, I was
so flattered that of course I said yes, I would. I knew he
had been married before and had kids and all, but I said
sure anyhow. Just didn't think about it.

"At the beginning, things were pretty good between us.
Except for the sex part. He always wanted to have sex,
almost every day. I never cared for it much but would let
him do whatever he wanted. After all, I was his wife. Other
times he would be real bossy. Tell me the food I was making was no good, and he wouldn't even eat it. He'd waste
perfectly good food and just push the plate back and storm
out of the house. He would find fault with how I kept the
house, what kind of clothes I wore, things like that. But
I don't mean to make it sound like it was all bad between
us. It wasn't. He worked steady and, except for sometimes when he would stop at the corner tavern, brought
all his money home for me and the kids. After a while,
though, he stopped having sex with me so frequently. I
figured that he was probably seeing somebody. I knew
I should have cared about that, but I really didn't. It was
almost a relief. I just never mentioned it, and he never
did either.

"By the time Eileen—she's the oldest—was about seven,
she and Frank used to spend a lot of time together. Always
laughing and teasing each other. Sometimes that would
make me mad, because he hardly ever did that with me
anymore, and other times I used to be glad Eileen was having a kind of relationship with her father that I never had.
So I was glad about that part of it. She was always such a
good girl. She always used to help me with the youngest
kids, just like I did when I was her age. She never seemed
to mind, and I guess I just gave her more and more to do.
It was rough for me to keep up with everything that had to
be done, you know?

"It's still so hard to come right out and say it. It makes

me feel so awful and so ashamed, that something like that could happen. I just wish I could cry, but it all feels so tight and locked up inside me that I can't.

"I suppose I first knew something was going on when I saw Eileen sitting on Frank's lap and he was telling her some joke and rubbing her leg, all up under her skirt and everything. He stopped right away when he saw me looking at them, but Eileen looked at me so cold and angry. She looked at me just like my mother used to when I was small. That look made me feel so bad that I just turned and went out of the room. I guess I knew something was going on that wasn't right, but I just made believe I hadn't seen it. I just didn't know what to do.

"Eileen kept away from me after that, and though she still helped me with the other kids and the house, she spent all her time in the evening with her father. Every time I looked up, they would be together, laughing, talking, telling jokes. I was always out of it.

"One day a teacher from school called and told me to come right over. I had this awful feeling in my stomach that something terrible was about to happen, and I went right over. I went to the principal's office and found out Eileen had told a girlfriend that she had been having sex with her father. The girlfriend told, and when they asked Eileen she denied it and started to cry. I sat there, feeling this big, cold lump in my stomach, feeling so ashamed. They were looking at me like I was some kind of bug in front of them on a microscope. They weren't mean or anything; they just made me feel like I wasn't the same kind of person they were. I told them I would go home and find out if it were true. I got out of there as fast as I could.

"When Frank came home that same night, I put it right to him. Just like they had said it in school. He denied it, but his face got all funny, and I had the feeling he was

lying. I went into Eileen's room and told her the same
thing, and she started to cry and denied it. I knew they
were both lying, and I hit her. God knows why I hit her
instead of him, but I did. I wanted to hug her and tell her
it would be alright, but instead I hit her.

"I went out into the living room and told Frank he better
be gone or I was going to call the police. He tried to talk to
me, and I just wouldn't listen. There was nothing he could
say to me that I wanted to hear."

Frank eventually was arrested, as Louise wanted him
to be, but she lost her daughter as well. The court decided
that Eileen should be placed in a foster home "for her
own protection."

Left with her three youngest children, Louise also became a victim. Alone, feeling betrayed by her husband and
further punished by a court system that has determined
that she is an "unfit mother," she repeatedly expressed
the wish to me that her daughter would "run away" from
her foster home and come back so they could be a "real
family again."

Louise, who was trained to be ashamed and embarrassed
about her own sexuality, who tried to provide a kind of
mothering for her daughter that she had never received as
a child and who was emotionally and financially dependent on her husband, feels that she has been punished for
something she didn't do: "It's hard to explain how a person can feel invisible in their own house, but that's how I
felt. I was the somebody who did the shopping, cooked
the meals, cleaned the house, ironed the clothes. But it was
always like they were looking right through me, like I
wasn't even there at all, like a machine. Maybe I would
have tried to talk if I felt that there was somebody who
was interested in listening."

But no one was there to listen to Louise. She, like many
other members of families in which incestuous assault

takes place, did not know how to or to whom she could
talk about her feelings.

Donna

Donna, a heavyset, stolid woman in her early forties, described the personal changes she experienced during her
married life, her horror upon discovering her husband's
sexual abuse of their daughter and the estrangement the
incestuous assault caused between herself and her child.
What emerged was a portrait of a woman who had tried
to create a more satisfying life for herself and who, in
that process, also became a victim.

"I was a good wife and mother when the girls were small.
I did nothing but stay home, pack lunches, prepare dinners, clean the house, car-pool. I was the real all-American
woman. It's not that John wasn't a good husband. He was.
We were happy in those years, or I thought we were then.
But, you know, after a while it gets hard to listen to everybody else's problems. Nobody ever assumed I had any of
my own. Or that I might be bored with doing the same
things over and over. I knew he wasn't being advanced at
the plant as fast as he should have been. I sympathized
with him when they kept bringing younger and younger
men in and putting them in jobs he should have had. I
tried to encourage him to go back to school to get his
diploma so he could have that piece of paper they felt he
needed. I used to talk myself blue in the face.
  "Trying to take care of everybody, except myself—that
gets to wear you down after a while. So I felt that if John
wouldn't go back to school, then I would. I had never had
a chance to finish school. I met John in college right in
the first semester of my freshman year. He was a junior
and, well, you know the story, we fell in love, were married
and I got pregnant right away. So he had to quit school
and went to work. He never complained about it then,

but in the last few years he started to talk about it and made it seem as though it was my fault that I got pregnant. Like it was something I could do alone, you know?

"Melody and her father were always close, and they had a wonderful relationship all the time she was growing up. He was a good father and always thought of her as his 'special princess.' Karen was the studious one, always stuck in her school books ever since she was small. She's more like me, I guess. But Melody and John were always together. Like sweethearts, I realize now looking back on it. Like real sweethearts.

"By the time Karen and Melody were twelve and fourteen, I just decided I had done all the time I was going to do without having something for myself. So I went back to the community college and started paying attention to myself a little more. I didn't spend so much time on the cleaning and the cooking as I had in the past and used most of my evenings to keep up with my schoolwork. It was one of the most exciting times of my life, although it sure didn't last too long.

"By that time John and I didn't have much of a sex life, but I thought that was natural. After all, for people like us, faithful to each other for all those years, sex gets dull after a while. I expect it does for lots of people. So when our activity started to fall off, I didn't really care much. It was alright with me. I never thought John was the kind of man to ever go out with another woman, so I figured that he was feeling as bored with the whole thing as I was.

"He sure didn't go out and find another woman. He slept with his own flesh and blood. How could I ever have imagined such a thing? Who would ever do something like that? It was going on right under my very nose, and I never suspected. Karen was finally the one who told me. She had heard them through the wall, in Melody's room, while I was down in the basement doing my homework. She didn't come right out and tell me. She waited a few days because she didn't know if she had really heard what she suspected. She asked Melody, who started to deny it but then admitted it and told her never to tell anybody. Especially me. But Karen and I are close, and she came right away to tell me.

"I can still remember sitting at the dinette set looking at my cup of coffee until it got so cold that a white glaze formed over the top of the cup. I just sat, not knowing what to do, what to say, where to go. It was like the bottom fell out of my world that morning."

Donna is in the process of divorcing John in ugly and acrimonious proceedings. She is trying to forbid him to have any contact with either daughter and is having her lawyers urge him to leave the state.

"I'm still left with the mopping up action. I'm always left with that. I guess women always are. Men make the mess and we stay behind to clean it up. Melody and I are going to see a woman therapist twice a week. Not a man, you can count on that. We each go alone once, and we go together once. She's sorry that it happened and misses her father very much. It nearly kills me to hear her say that, after what he did. But she still loves him. She never wanted to have sex with him, but she says in the therapy sessions that she felt so sorry for him, and he pressured her so much, that she just did. They both felt like I had abandoned them and didn't care about anybody but myself, and all they had was each other. John was never the sort of man to have many friends. He would go to work and come home and putter around the house. So they felt they could only turn to each other.

"It can make you bitter thinking about it. I don't know if I will ever be able to forgive Melody for what she did. I'm hoping the therapy will help me learn to do that and learn to love her again, but it's still hard. Every time I look at her it's like tearing open a big wound that doesn't heal."

In nearly all the families I interviewed, there was a painful estrangement between the mother and her victimized

109

daughter. These breakdowns in mother/daughter relationships came about in a number of ways. In some homes the mothers were partially or totally physically handicapped; other mothers had recurring histories of mental illness and either lived within their homes as invalids or frequently were absent from them during periods of hospitalization. Some were borderline alcoholics, while others simply chose to recede into the background of family life by withdrawing emotionally, taking jobs or becoming involved in activities that took them out of the home for long intervals.

Many incest victims were extremely vocal about the rift between themselves and their mothers. Edith's mother had repeated mental breakdowns while Edith was growing up: "I knew Mom couldn't help it, getting sick that way. But it always fell on me every time she went away to take care of everything. And as it turned out, everything was really the right word."

Sharon's mother went to work when Sharon was still very young because her husband was a chronic alcoholic and she needed to augment his income to keep the family intact. "My father was a real bastard," Sharon related, "coming home drunk and raging around the place every night. But I hardly ever got to see my mother. She got up when it was still dark and went to work, and came home when it was already starting to get dark again, after taking three buses home. When my father started being sexual with me, I just couldn't tell her. It would have killed her. I felt like it was my job to protect her because she had so much to put up with as it was. Any more would have been just too much. I just could never understand why she continued to stay with him, why she kept making excuses and hoping he would change. That's most of all what made me mad. If she had just thrown him out like she should have years before, none of this would have happened. She should have just thrown him out."

the mothers

Josie remembered a similar childhood: "My father was an animal. He used to push my mother around, and she would never say anything. She would sort of duck her head and never answer him back. When he would get off into a rage, there was nothing else to do. So when he started to push me around and touch me under my skirt, I just never felt like I had anybody to tell. My mother had never fought him, so I surely wasn't going to be able to."

Not all victims remember violent or alcoholic homes. Catherine told me, "My mother got a job when I was ten. She was always saying she was tired of being stuck in the four walls all the time. My father always laughed at her, telling her that she couldn't do anything that anybody was going to pay for, and besides her job was in her own home. Well, finally she just went ahead and got a job in a notions store. It took me many years to really understand how hard that must have been for her to do and how that was about the only rebellious thing she ever could manage. But when she started to work, I was the one who had to pre-pare dinner, I was the one who had to see to the laundry, I was the one who spent the evenings stuck with him while she went into her room and went to bed because she was so tired.

"It's like she just couldn't find a way to manage to pro-tect herself and protect me, too. So she did what she could to be her own person as well as she could figure that out. I used to blame her, though. I used to feel that if she had stayed at home, like a 'real' mother, that my father wouldn't have been sexual with me. In a real backwards way, I made her responsible for what he did."

Catherine is not alone in blaming her mother. The mothers in incest families frequently are blamed by their husbands, and all too often they blame themselves as well.

Many mothers painfully remember their daughters trying to tell them of their victimization at the hands of their fathers or stepfathers. One woman, now a participant in a counseling group for mothers of incest victims, described her daughter's behavior in a sorrowful and halting mono-tone: "Barbara always used to take baths. From the time she was very small, every time I can remember, I heard the bathtub being filled up. She would sometimes take two or three baths a day. I used to holler at her for wasting so much water and sometimes, when I was at my wits' end, would hit her and forbid her to bathe. Even then she would keep washing her hands, over and over, scrubbing her hands like she wanted to get something off them. I didn't understand what she was trying to tell me. How could I have known such a thing? I blame myself for that, though. She was too afraid to tell me straight out and was doing the only thing she could think of to let me know. And I didn't listen. At least we have been able to talk about it now. The therapy has brought it all out in the open, and she forgives me for not understanding. But it's hard for me to forgive myself. Even now."

Another woman who is receiving counseling to try to come to terms with her painful feelings about her child's victimization described her daughter's physical symptoms: "Maria was always complaining of stomach aches. But when I would ask her where it hurt, she would always point to a place way down near her privates. I would tell her that wasn't her stomach, but she would insist and cry that it hurt. When I would take her to the pediatrician for checkups, she would tell him, too, and he would press her stomach and abdomen and ask her exactly where it hurt. She would never show him but just repeat that it hurt all the time. It never occurred to him, or to me for that matter, to examine her genitals or her pelvic area. After all, she was only nine or ten years old. So I finally just told her to stop complaining about imaginary things and to get her mind off it. She did, after a time, stop complaining, and I never knew what the real cause of her stomach aches was until she became pregnant at thirteen. Then it all came out, and I realized she had been trying to tell me all along and was afraid to hurt me because she knew how much I loved her daddy. She was protecting me, and I should have been the one to protect her." The woman began to cry softly. She turned her head away and whispered, "It's a lot of guilt for me to bear, and I don't know if I can ever rid myself of it."

Blame is placed on mothers by still another group. The professional community has developed theories which place considerable responsibility on the mother for the incestuous assault having taken place. One theory posits that the mother identifies with her child and in so doing is, in fantasy, gratifying her childhood incestuous desire for her own father. Another theory reverses the above analysis and suggests that in cases in which the mother has some knowledge that the incestuous assault is occurring and has fostered a pseudomaturity in her child, she is actually setting the stage for the incest in order to act out a dependent relationship she may never have had with her own mother, with her daughter assuming the mother's role.

Boxed in on both sides, mothers are seen as either living out a fantasy never explored with their fathers or as seeking out a relationship they never had with their mothers. The box becomes even smaller when theorists accuse these women of having "deserted" their husbands emotionally and sexually, thus forcing their children to assume that role. According to these theorists, the forms of "desertion" include a mother's taking a job, developing an outside interest, having another child or being emotionally or physically unable to assume the wife/mother role she is "supposed" to assume.

The two words which consistently intrude upon all theory and analysis concerning mothers in families in which incestuous assault occurs are "abandoning" and "colluding." These are the names of their crimes, the reasons they are held responsible for the actions of others. If a mother is "passive," she fails by not having provided her child with the strength to resist incestuous overtures. If she is "aggressive," she fails by having caused her husband to feel emasculated and therefore in need of turning to someone else for his emotional and sexual needs.

In this kind of analysis it is assumed and seldom questioned that the adult male could not, or would not, turn to his child for his sexual needs, nor would the child feel constrained to acquiesce to his demands, if the mother in the family had not precipitated the emotional climate by the crimes of commission and omission for which she is judged guilty. And she becomes guilty, too, upon public knowledge of the incestuous abuse by being more hostile to, and non-supportive of, her child than the aggressor.

In addition to theories placing blame on the mothers of incest victims, the professional community has developed profiles of these women. One such profile tells us that they are dependent, infantile, often pathologically attached to their own mothers and prone to panic in the face of responsibility.[1] However, there are many reasons why such women are inadequate as parents, and rather than perpetuating the guilt and blame that further heighten their feelings of culpability, a different kind of analysis is needed to shed some light on the emotional tightropes they walk. If they are immature and dependent, we need to find out how they became that way.

Many mothers of incest victims were themselves victims of physical or sexual abuse as children. If they never received the mothering they needed when they were children, they may not have the skill or experience necessary to provide love and protection for their own children. Having been rejected by their own mothers, some women reverse the parenting roles and turn to their children for the mothering they still so desperately need for themselves.

Other women are unwilling or unable to give their daughters a childhood they never had. Although our motherhood

the mothers

mythology tells women that it is deeply satisfying to work hard and sacrifice to provide their children with options they themselves never had, in fact such sacrifices cause many mothers to become resentful. I have been told by countless women what was most clearly expressed by a woman who has two teenage daughters: "Sure, I love my kids, and I'd do anything for them. But there are times I resent the fact that they have a patient and sacrificing and understanding mother. I never had that, and it makes me mad that they have something I still wish I could have had with my own mother. I suppose it sounds like a contradiction, and it is, but there are times when I feel my tit is sucked dry and I have no place to go to get what I need for myself."

Still other women are sexually naive or uninformed and have no options available to understand the source of their sexual dysfunction; so they withdraw from their husbands to avoid the confusion and disgust their sexuality causes them. Often married to brutal or unaffectionate sexual partners, they are held responsible for their spouses' actions because they have held back from sexual activity with men who confirm their earliest fears that sex is ugly, unfeeling or a source of conflict and tension. Although it is consistently true of families in which incestuous assault takes place that the sexual relationship between husband and wife is either strained or non-existent, society seems ready to accept a wife's sexual problems as a valid "reason" why a father might turn to his daughter to get what is his "right."

It is more to the point to ask ourselves why a man, given an unsatisfactory sexual relationship with his wife, makes the damaging choice of his own child as a sexual surrogate. Part of what men have been conditioned to expect within their families is the nurturing and attention their central position as an adult male affords them. When their wives do not fulfill their expectations, instead of examining their expectations or exploring their feelings with their wives,

115

many turn to other females in the family for the satisfaction of their needs. Because women are expected to meet the emotional, sexual and physical needs of their men as dictated by their societal roles, any abdication of this role by the wife most often is viewed as rejection of the husband and pathological behavior proving the woman to be "unfit," "unhealthy" or "immature."

Much of the bedrock upon which such traditional beliefs rest is composed of culturally conditioned, unexamined premises—premises in which we all have much invested. Our homes are thought of as our private castles, within which the roles of king and queen have been culturally defined and have remained greatly unchanged in the transition from the larger, more extended families of the past to today's smaller, isolated nuclear units. Within this family unit, a woman is expected to enthusiastically fulfill her husband's needs, raise and socialize their offspring to continue to play out similar roles and, at all costs, remain nurturing, loving and accessible to all members of the family. Except herself.

A woman's loving concern for herself often is seen as an abandonment of her family. A woman is not free to acknowledge her interests and her hungers and to attempt to act upon them in a self-actualizing way. She also is not free to be enraged, in pain, confused or ambivalent about any of her socially assigned tasks, for that is seen as a denial of her central role as a woman. She must not neglect her family's needs; she must not take a job; she must not become emotionally unstable, physically unwell, angry or disinterested in her duties. For if she does, and her family disintegrates, the full weight of the responsibility rests on her betrayal of her role—a rigid role which leaves her little room to grow and develop freely, honestly and without great cost. Thus, because most of our society continues to define a "normal" woman as one who fulfills her job as a wife and mother in a consistent and competent manner, women who cannot meet traditional responsibilities because they are suffering emotionally or physically, or who choose to withdraw from those responsibilities for whatever reason, are made to carry the burden of guilt for the emotional disruption that may result from their abdication.

Many people in our culture fail to see that a great number of women who take jobs out of the house, return to school, develop outside interests or start to grow less dependent on their husbands are beginning to display new and necessary signs of health in their development as autonomous beings. Such behavior is more indicative of personal growth than abandonment. If women need to move toward their own lives, it is inevitable that they will, for a time at least, move away from the lives of others who have come to be personally and culturally dependent upon them. Such changes might very well be embraced optimistically, rather than being looked upon as destructive, for they signal the possibility of a more human definition of family roles permitting each family member greater opportunity for personal growth and satisfaction both within and outside the family unit.

It is not only the mothers in incest families who have to deal with feelings of jealousy, competitiveness, self-denial and powerlessness. In the endlessly shifting balance of relationships within all families, such feelings are experienced by many mothers.

One middle-class mother, traditional in her values, speaks for many:

"It's hard for me to admit, but there's a real element of jealousy involved. I had a couple of boyfriends before I got married, but you couldn't by any stretch of the imagination call me a sexually experienced woman. Bill and I have been married for fifteen years, and I have been faithful to him for all of that time. It crossed my mind a few times, like it does with everyone, but it's a solid relationship and I just never wanted to risk it for the sake of experimenting. So I just stuck pretty close to home sexually. Bill was much more experienced than I when we got married, but it was experience in a vacuum, if you know what I mean. He had never really loved anybody he had sex with. It was just detached.

"We've made a good marriage, he and I. Have two great kids—Tim is eleven and is his father's spitting image. He's on the Little League team this summer—Bill coaches them in the evenings and on Saturdays—and I've been working part-time in the real-estate office in town so we can get a college fund together for both the children.

"I guess we're pretty normal. We talk about most things and share most of the same goals together. It's really only been in the last year or so that this friction has begun between Kathy and me. She's fourteen now, and she developed real early. I did, too, but times were so different then. She wears tiny halters and tiny shorts, and the boys are all starting to sniff around her. It makes me uncomfortable, and I just don't know how to handle it.

"Bill is a very attentive father to Kathy. She's our first born. He always left the every-day part of her raising to me. I helped her with her schoolwork, told her about menstruation and babies, planned the birthday parties. That's a mother's responsibility, I suppose. He was more involved with Tim than with Kathy, and I felt that was only natural.

"It's hard to explain what I'm feeling about Kathy, but there's something about seeing your own baby, all developed like a woman, beginning to go out with boys. It seems as though there is a distance growing between us and we don't ever seem to talk to each other. Her friends are the most important people to her now, and she just flies in and out of the house to eat and sleep. There are times when I sit across the table from her watching her eat and try to remember when she was my baby, and find myself looking at a person I don't really know anymore.

the mothers

"As much as Kathy and I seem to have grown apart in the last year or two, she seems to be getting closer with Bill. He always tells her she reminds him of me when we got married, and she loves it. I don't love it, I can tell you that. How do you think that makes me feel? Like some outsider, an outsider in my own family.

"I don't want Kathy to be a reproduction of me, but I want her to know me. I want to be able to tell her what it was like for me when I was her age, how much I understand of what she's experiencing and how much I don't understand. I want us to take walks together and laugh and tell secrets. Not like mother and daughter, but like two women. But I don't know how."

Many women feel like outsiders in their own homes, wanting to reach out but feeling awkward and uncertain about how to begin. Relationships change, and oftentimes women silently watch the shifting and then turn away. They do not turn away in silence, however; often there is a deep and searing rage that is rooted in their not knowing how to make anything different.

The voices of incest victims' mothers echo the estrangement many women feel from their dreams and expectations and the sharing and closeness they had anticipated in their marriages, as well as their competitive and awkward feelings about their children. The result is a message many mothers—not just those of incest victims—send to their children as they try to meet the demands placed on them as wives and mothers: "Your father first and you second. It would be too dangerous to fight back, because if I lose him, I lose everything. For my own survival I must leave you to your devices. I cannot defend you, and if necessary I will sacrifice you to your father."[2]

The mothers of incest victims are dependent on their husbands, and some, unable to acknowledge that their partners have abused their children, become invested in a self-protective way in not knowing. For if they know, they will

be required to act in ways that threaten the very underpin-
nings of their lives. This kind of denial is predicated on a
wisely perceived estimate of what is at risk. Some women
who are aware of the abuse do not and will not talk about
it so that it will "go away" sooner and cease to frighten
them. Others, anxious and fearful about what their friends
and neighbors will say, become immobilized, needing help
but not knowing where to turn.

A counselor in one of the few programs set up to work
with incest families confirms this view of victims' mothers.
Often, she says, mothers are afraid of being beaten, afraid
of the loss of family security, afraid of their families being
broken up, afraid of not knowing where to go and what's
going to happen. And, along with their paralyzing fears,
they come to carry feelings of guilt and responsibility for
having ignored the abuse and its consequences.

The weight and sudden revelation of the incestuous assault
paralyzes other mothers, and their feelings of frustration
and powerlessness often are turned upon their children in
anger, blame or dismissal of the effects of the abuse, thus
heightening the victims' confusion and exacerbating the
estrangement between mother and child. Such a defensive
response by the mother is compounded when the aggressor
is her husband or partner and she feels she must choose between keeping her family intact and protecting her child.

Sally remembered her mother's confusion and denial
after she already had called the police to report Sally's
father. When it was explained that she would have to press
charges and that her husband most likely would go to jail,
Sally's mother reconsidered.

"I guess Mom only called the police because she wanted
to be sure my dad stopped," Sally explained. "She just
didn't know that wasn't how it worked. By the time they
got through explaining the examination, the hearings and
the trial, she just couldn't face going through with it. And
she told them to never mind, she would handle it herself."

the mothers

Sally's mother did "handle it." Feeling guilty about permitting her husband to remain in their home, even after his repeated assurances that the sexual assaults would not reoccur, she reacted defensively by insisting to Sally that what had happened wasn't really so bad, that it wasn't "the end of the world"—"Daddy is dreadfully sorry, and it will never happen again." Thereafter, Sally was not permitted to talk about her trauma, ask questions about it or express her feelings about it; for her mother needed to believe that the incestuous assault had not been damaging or traumatic in order to convince herself that she had made the right decision in not seeking legal or psychological intervention.

A mother's denial of the assault and its effects on her child may stem from other sources. Many women feel a deep sense of loyalty to their husbands, who provide financially for them, who may have rescued them from abusive or emotionally barren homes, who are hardworking and loyal and who gave them their first sense of belonging and acceptance in the world. With other women, the denial is motivated by self-doubt. Unable to believe their suspicions could be correct, unable to stand up to their husbands, unable to extricate themselves from feelings of jealousy or competitiveness with their daughters, they turn away.

Sylvia, a weary mother of four, cut through all the theory and analysis and asked, "What do these damn fools expect me to do? Sure Tommy is a no-good. Don't think I haven't known that for years. I never expected anything like this, though. But now that it's happened, I can't even say I'm surprised. Women are all the same to him. It doesn't matter much as long as he gets to have sex when he wants it. It never seems to matter what the woman wants. Once the feeling comes over him, he can't think about anything else."

Sylvia's husband had just been arrested for sexually molesting their two oldest daughters. I was present as the child-protection services worker assigned to the case urged

121

conspiracy of silence

Sylvia to press charges and have him sent to jail. She was intent on convincing Sylvia that if her husband were not locked up, he would repeat his behavior with other young girls in the neighborhood. Sylvia listened patiently to all the arguments marshalled by this young woman, then turned to me and said:

"This is the first damn time I ever had a home of my own. Never even had a room of my own when I was growing up, never had my own clothes, always wore hand-me-downs. My two girls are no good. Never have been any good. They've both been with all the boys on the block by now, I'll bet. I've never been able to control either of them. Just always knew their own minds and went ahead and did what they damn well wanted to. Now, don't misunderstand me, I'm not saying what Tommy did was right, or making excuses for him. But I have to think about myself, too. Who the hell is going to take care of me and the kids if I put him in jail? Who's going to hire me? A fat, tired, broken-down woman without a skill to her name. What am I supposed to do? Be a maid like my mama before me? I decided when I left home I was never going to be nobody's maid, and I haven't changed my mind one bit.

"I didn't mean to give that social worker such a hard time. I knew what she was trying to tell me. The problem is, she didn't know what I was trying to tell her. There were eight kids in my home, and my mama never saw the money to buy clothes and food for us all the time we were small. My father hardly ever could find work. Sometimes he would try, but most of the time he would get angry and drunk and hit whoever was in his sight. I was the oldest one and I learned pretty quick to keep out of his way, but he left me with some scars. Both inside and outside.

"But all the time, I knew I wasn't going to have a life like that when I left home. And Tommy's coming up wasn't much easier than mine. In fact, he still has the mark of a hot iron on his back from his father, who was a real violent man. You have to understand that Tommy's all I got. I know what he did was bad, but he's my husband and I don't want to put him in jail. I'd rather work it out among us. I don't know exactly how to do that—talking about sex is not an easy thing for me to do—but a family has to try to work things out together. And he's so ashamed, he feels so bad, that we have a chance."

Some mothers do act—out of a strength born of desperation. Loretta pressed charges against her husband when his incestuous assaults were uncovered as a result of a routine examination of her daughters at a pediatric clinic. Sending her husband to jail and going on welfare was a welcome relief from the increasing abuse she had become resigned to expect from her husband.

"He's a very violent man," Loretta explained. "From the beginning, whenever he got mad at anything, he would punch or kick it. He broke the television because he couldn't get a clear picture. He was the same with me. If I did something he didn't like—and believe me, I tried never to do that—he would just pop me one. We were all living on top of each other in that little place, and nobody ever had a corner that was their own. So the kids saw everything that happened. He was so big, and I never had anybody to go to; so I just tried to keep out of his way.

"When we got married, I really thought it was going to be like in the magazines. I would make nice dinners and keep the house and have babies for him. That's how it was supposed to be. But that's only in the magazines. From the very first, that never worked out right.

"I did leave once and took the kids to my mother's, but she didn't have any room for me and three little ones. She had all she could do to look after my younger brothers and sisters. So we just came back home, had nowhere else to go. But now that Donald has had sex with Billie, I just have to put an end to it. Once and

123

for all. I just can't go on like this; it's no kind of life. It's not even like being alive most of the time."

Loretta's hoped-for satisfaction as a wife and mother had been quickly nullified by her husband's brutality. In the face of his increasingly deviant behavior, she became emotionally immobilized. Billie felt she had no choice but to submit to her father since she did not see her mother as a source of protection from his abuse. Unable over the years to pretend to herself that her husband was going to live up to the romantic illusions she had brought to her early marriage, Loretta had transferred all her feelings of love and caring to her eldest daughter. She finally was able to free herself from the apathy and despair that had defined most of her life and made a choice for the safety and well-being of her child. But by the time she made that choice, much of the damage already had been done. It is easier for Loretta and Billie now, because although they are both in a great deal of pain and feel a sense of loss, Billie feels protected and cared for by her mother, and Loretta is finally exercising her strength to make decisions about her own life.

In her pamphlet dealing with the sexual abuse of children within the family, Yvonne Tormes offers a more human analysis of the mothers of incest victims than has been made in the past. She notes that in addition to a lack of faith in helping agencies, these women may be inhibited from seeking help by an inability to admit their husband's guilt; such a defensive response is aimed at justifying their choice of spouse and warding off ego-shattering experiences. Tormes also writes of their fears: fear of not being able to handle such an enormous problem alone, fear of financial problems that will result if their husbands (often the only wage-earners) are removed from the home; fear of brutal retaliation by husbands if they report the offenses; fear of stigmatizing the family in the eyes of the community and fear of becoming entangled with the law and its terrifying labyrinth of agencies.[3]

the mothers

In spite of these very real threats to their well-being, such mothers receive little or no sympathy from the professional community. The majority still view them as cold, harsh, unloving, rejecting, moralistic, overly religious and/or helpless. Having buried them beneath this barrage of labels, professionals rarely see these women in the very real context of their lives. Few seem to recognize that if a mother behaves in an unloving way toward her children, it may be because her cultural oppression has diminished her capacity for expressing love. A mother's anger at her children often is rooted in a hostility toward society arising from her role as a woman and results from the fact that she has no other options for releasing her anger.

Again and again we see the victimization of the mothers of incest victims. What choices have many had? How are they to understand how to provide a loving and nurturing framework in which their children can grow and flourish when they did not have such experiences themselves? How can they acknowledge their children's needs when they were taught to suppress and deny their own? How can they provide "resistive personality traits" when they never learned to develop any for themselves? How can they present role models for their children to emulate when they are unable to control the forces threatening their own lives?

Perhaps some can reach out for support and strength to deal with this painful problem, but many others do not know how to begin. The responsibility lies with us to create a bridge so that other women do not have to experience emotional isolation, do not have to unquestioningly accept society's unrealistic expectations of them and can become clear about their right to their own power—a bridge over which women and their families can cross into a more positive and loving future.

THE FAMILY

♦♦♦♦♦♦♦♦♦

The American family, caught in the midst of pressures, tensions and redefinition, is the primary place in which all of us learn our earliest lessons about intimacy. Although these lessons frequently are not verbalized or consciously transmitted, they are central life experiences and leave an indelible mark on growing children.

In the transition from the extended families of our recent past to the more insulated and isolated nuclear family units in which we now live, we have gained little and paid dearly. We all are dependent on one another to satisfy our emotional, physical and social needs. However, the nuclear family alone cannot provide all of these resources and thus forces many of us into a social and emotional isolation with few outlets for the anger, tension and aggressive feelings that may result from our unfulfilled needs. Furthermore, we are in a period when the significance of the family and the role it is expected to play are no longer clear, and we are trying to redefine the nuclear family structure and create alternatives to it. In moving away from a time when rigid societal attitudes dictated what our roles were to be as men and women and what was required of us as parents, we are experiencing uncertainty in determining new roles for ourselves. Many of us feel we have stumbled into a time when few of the old rules still apply while a frightening number of options and choices have become available to us, and we find ourselves floundering among all these choices, growing increasingly uncertain and confused.

As we close one cycle in our history and begin a new one, we are finding few if any guidelines with which to shape and define our future. There are no more absolutes, no more right or wrong, and we are experiencing a tumultuous period of "personal growth," "self-discovery" and "human potential." Although it is premature to assess precisely what all these changes will contribute to the quality of our lives, it is certainly time to look at what price we are paying for many of our new "freedoms."

Surrounded by innumerable choices and their concomitant responsibility, many men and women are harboring the same expectations of and making the same demands upon their new lifestyles as they had made upon older and more traditional ways of life. Whether we live in single-parent families, nuclear families or extended communal families, we expect that the family, in whatever form, will provide us with all that we cannot find elsewhere. We hope it will give us a sense of belonging and that it will be a place where we can communicate openly and honestly, a place where our needs for sex and intimacy will be fulfilled.

Most people begin by choosing a partner to "love and cherish" who has been picked largely on the basis of whatever emotional baggage we are carrying as a result of our early life experiences. Although it is becoming increasingly common for men and women to marry out of their social class, religious affiliation and racial background, rarely do we marry someone far removed from our own sense of self-esteem. We pick partners who reflect our images of

127

ourselves, and we fervently hope these mates will help to make us feel "whole."

Although more and more women are beginning the difficult and painful work of stripping away the illusions that led them to make their marital choices and are struggling to find more satisfying lifestyles, it is a slow and terribly painful process. During such transition periods the reasons some marriages are dissolved may be as thoughtless as the reasons for which they were begun. But for a while, at least, such experiences are inevitable.

And what of men in this time of transition, women's liberation, growing unemployment and changing values? It is no longer clear, as it was twenty years ago, what it means to be a man or a woman, what it means to be married and what the guidelines are for raising a child. Being a man doesn't mean the same things as it used to, and it is unclear precisely what it does mean. No longer necessarily the breadwinner, the economic bulwark of the family group, the man's role is changing. More and more women are entering the work force, both to augment the family income and to stretch their own life experiences beyond the limited confines of the home. If a man is no longer supposed to be the provider, the head of the household, the stabilizing patriarchal force as he has been in the past, then what on earth is he supposed to be?

The feminist movement is providing some women with new role definitions, but there is very little of this kind of support and guidance available to men. Most men are unable to voice what it is that they feel has been taken from them, but they clearly sense that something is gone—something solid, tangible and safe. A way of life.

And what about having children? Bearing and raising children is considered one of the most important and greatest tasks of our lives. In our culture women are expected to have a "natural" surging of maternal instinct, which is expected to provide them with guidelines for successful

mothering. When a mother performs the duties which
society defines as "naturally" hers, she is seen as being
a "good" parent. Although women presumably have access
to a maternal instinct, there is no such cultural assumption
of a paternal instinct. Furthermore, men are not considered
unfulfilled if they remain childless, and they are not expected to possess a mysterious wellspring of "intuitive"
processes that will aid them in parenting.

For most of us, parenting entails devotion, concern, guilt,
ambivalence and anxiety for at least twenty years of our
lives. We do this with no training, except for the societal
values we are implicitly expected to know and to pass on,
in hopes of producing "happy" children and consequently
considering ourselves to be "good" parents. In parenting,
men and women may carry into their families unfinished
business from their own childhood pasts. In these cases,
parents often turn to their children to act out their own
unresolved dramas. Ways of relating to one another also
are passed on from generation to generation. For many
people today, family socialization patterns remain much
as they were twenty or thirty years ago primarily because
today's mothers and fathers have learned how to be parents as a result of the care—good or bad—they received
from their own parents a generation earlier.

In examining our early childhood socialization and the
changes and confusion evident in our culture today, we
can discover some of the dynamics underlying incestuous
abuse.

Mothers are the first human beings children experience
and from whom they learn that emotional bonding is to be
eagerly sought and joyously shared while sexual bonding is
forbidden. In order to earn their mothers' love, children
learn to repress their own instinctive sexuality. Most come
to understand that certain parts of the body are touched
and stroked in a loving and caring way while others are not

129

to be displayed or talked about. Children also learn that touching, fondling and curiosity about their own erogenous areas are forbidden and shameful activities. It is not surprising, then, that most of us reach adulthood viewing our genitalia as "other" than us, the only parts of our bodies that are not totally ours, but instead are governed by a silent and powerful set of rules that nobody quite explains.

A mother is taught that it is important for her son to give up his attachment to her and to identify with his father or father figure, who is seen as powerful. Males represent not only the authority of the family, but of the culture itself, and as part of a boy child's socialization, he is required to turn away from his first source of nurturing, acceptance and love and identify with those whose bodies are like his and who are representatives of the dominant culture.

What is the price boys pay for this turning away? Often the most damaging result is that they learn to distrust and deny everything feminine in themselves. Their need for non-sexual physical intimacy and hunger for nurturance, expressiveness and tenderness cannot be acknowledged or gratified in the service of their development into "real little men." Socialized by fathers who were taught to distrust and feel contemptuous of the female characteristics in their own mothers and in themselves, many young men join male society at the price of denying their needs to feel safe, loving and close to another person without pretense, posture or outright dishonesty. Because they are raised in a culture that stresses competitiveness, achievement and power for them, their roles and options often become calcified as they get older. Their sexuality may become inextricably bound up in conquering one who is weaker and less powerful than they, and they may find it difficult to develop true intimacy in their relationships with others.

In our society men have been expected to provide for their families and to maintain their role as powerful head of the household. In living up to societal expectations, most men

the family

do not permit themselves to express their emotions and are distrustful of the imagined weakness in real caring. Many define strength as force, flexibility as a sign of weakness and open dialogue as not knowing their own mind and view their wives and children as their possessions and responsibility.

And what of our daughters? Much as boys are trained into the world of their fathers, girls are as intensively socialized as were their mothers toward a prescribed life goal of marriage. Although in more and more homes today lip service is being paid to a number of alternative lifestyles, the pressure exerted on girls and their mothers to fulfill conventional sex-role expectations is still powerful and central.

Girls are taught from birth that they are unable to analyze and are intuitive, overemotional, passive, physically weak and dependent by nature. Furthermore, in learning to become women, young girls are barraged with an endless series of double messages. From the day a young girl begins to perceive what is expected of her, she receives a series of contradictory instructions about the way she is supposed to look and behave. She must be both sexy and a virgin, appreciative yet challenging, dependent but not clinging, vulnerable but able to protect herself, smart enough to get a man but not smart enough to threaten him—or at least smart enough to conceal her intelligence and act manipulatively.

Young girls are trained to adapt themselves to male needs by behaving in non-aggressive, non-competitive, compliant and passive ways. Their feelings of aggressiveness are severely controlled and punished. They are taught to suppress their anger and are conditioned to seek the comfort and reassurance they need from others rather than developing their own self-confidence. Above all, they learn to feel whole only when involved in interpersonal relationships with men.

conspiracy of silence

Women, trained to feel dependent, weak, vulnerable and fearful of abandonment, have learned to disguise their true feelings and abilities by outwardly behaving in the manner they have been raised to emulate. Such behavior is an adaptive response necessary for survival in a social environment which women rightly perceive as hostile to any behavior outside of the conventionally prescribed norm.

As a result of their childhood socialization, both men and women struggle with undoing their shame and ignorance about their sexuality—especially the passivity and silence with which many women still deal with sexual feelings and the detached and impersonal way many men deal with sexual relationships. As long as we remain equally victimized in our socialization, we are doomed to pass on unhealthy sexual attitudes to our children. Until sexual roles become more humanized, how can a man and a woman become truly intimate with each other when the impenetrable wall of custom and role expectations make it impossible for them to even see themselves and each other clearly?

Few parents feel comfortable with their own sexuality, much less the sexuality of their children. Researchers in the field of human sexuality have found that most parents were not satisfied with their personal sex education. Even more significantly, in many studies of marital relationships, partners frequently indicate that their sexual conflicts and problems are serious enough to threaten the foundation of their marriage.

Even now, in this period of presumed sexual openness, young people still obtain most of their information about sex and sexuality from magazines, movies and their friends, rather than from their parents. They find it difficult to ask intimate and troubling questions because they sense, and are put off by, the discomfort their parents are feeling. Thus our failure to acknowledge or openly discuss

the family

the sexuality that is such a central part of all our family lives and parenting becomes a clear sign to our children that certain feelings are to be avoided, certain questions are not to be asked, certain places are not to be touched and certain words are not to be said.

Our failure to acknowledge sexuality within the family also is indicative of a more basic discomfort; for there is a very real, ever-present fear in the minds of many parents that if they permit themselves to be honest and open sexual beings in their homes, that if they touch their children in a loving and nurturing manner, the only possible outcome will be sexual. The thought hovers, almost tangible, "If I touch you, I will feel or be sexual with you." And because of that fear, the most tender and basic expression of human love—physical closeness—may be denied within the family structure.

The difficulty parents and children share in communicating about sexuality stems from many sources. As parents, we are the first and primary source of sexual information for our children. However, some parents hesitate to initiate discussions of sexuality with their children because they feel they don't know enough. Although basic information concerning reproduction, contraception and venereal disease is readily available in any bookstore or library, many parents feel uncomfortable admitting, "I don't know. Let's look it up together." Other parents avoid confidential talks for fear they will appear old-fashioned, too conservative, not modern enough for their younger generation.

Another problem which further discourages parent/child communication is that while young people may find it difficult to relate to their parents as sexual beings like themselves, parents find it equally difficult to see their adolescent offspring as anything *but* sexual. Many adults are afraid that if sex information is made available to their children, experimentation immediately will follow. Most often, however, it is ignorance that stimulates much of premature adolescent sexual experimentation, not knowledge.

When sexuality is brought up among family members, establishing rules, rather than engaging in open dialogue, remains the unfortunate norm. Recent studies suggest that family communication about sexuality most often is characterized by the exercise of authority and rulemaking as opposed to verbal exploration of values in an atmosphere of cooperative disagreement. The rules often are as necessary for the emotional equilibrium of the parents as they are presumed necessary for the child's "proper" development.

Since there is no mutually shared language through which parents can express their feelings about sexuality to their children, young people consequently tend to feel inhibited when discussing their sexual feelings with their parents. Adolescents consider their parents to be much more sexually conservative than parents report themselves to be. This mutual denial and discomfort with each other's sexuality precludes the possibility of real and open communication between parents and children, and information that, if shared, could provide insight becomes unavailable to both.

If, for whatever reason, parents are uncomfortable with discussions of sexuality, their tension becomes apparent to their children, and an unspoken message is transmitted: "Some questions cannot be asked because they make Mommy and Daddy uncomfortable." Therefore, as the moments of discomfort, awkwardness and embarrassing attempts at communication accumulate over the years, with no opportunity for children to see their parents outside of the safe, circumscribed roles they have chosen to maintain with their offspring, children learn how to become parents who repeat similar unhealthy patterns with their own young.

Sol Gordon, Professor of Child and Family Studies at Syracuse University in New York, has distilled much of this into one question: "How can we ask children to be responsible for their behavior—sexual and otherwise—if we allow, and indeed guarantee, their ignorance by continuing to resist telling them the truth about themselves and about life in general?"[1]

But it is not only that parents feel uncomfortable about verbally and physically expressing themselves, their experiences and their feelings to their children. Parents also find it difficult to answer questions or set an example because the very nature of sexuality often is deeply troubling to them. The distinction between sexuality and the need for intimacy with another person proves especially difficult for many of us to work out. Often we enter sexual relationships with the expectation and illusion that our partners will be able to fulfill our more intense needs for closeness and acceptance. Hemmed in and pursued by the sexual pandering of media advertising, we barter our genitalia again and again, with a frail and fading hope that we will somehow achieve the total closeness and merging of spirit we sense can be found with another human being.

Attaining true intimacy with another person is a painfully difficult, time-consuming process which poses risks not necessarily present in sexual relationships. In becoming intimate, we allow ourselves to be vulnerable, to trust, to open fully to another person. However, some of us have so carefully protected ourselves from being hurt that we find it difficult to let down our barriers.

Many of us also find that we are estranged from our own sexuality. We are caught in a culture that makes use of our sexuality to move products off the shelves. Thus, having lost touch with our sexual nature, we are conditioned to buy back our sexuality in gaudy jars, perfume bottles, satin sheets and love oils. Innumerable books propose to teach us, step-by-step, how to be good lovers, how to be sexual gymnasts, how to understand and overcome our sexual dysfunction. Our sexuality has become simply another retailed commodity and source of ego gratification, and the chasm between this type of sex and real

conspiracy of silence

intimacy yawns wider with each emotional compromise.

In the same way that we purchase products that purport
to enhance our sex lives, many of us also are caught up in
displaying carefully tailored, painfully false attitudes of
sexual freedom. We demonstrate how we can touch everybody, kiss everybody and make love with everybody as a
way of proving our imagined sexual liberation. However,
it is much easier to have intercourse than it is to truly love.
Having frequent and detached sex can be one of the most
successful defenses against being close, for it takes enormous courage to become open and vulnerable with another
person for whom we are learning to care.

Although expressed sexual behavior appears to have
altered during recent years, perhaps all we are seeing is
the flip side of the coin. In our not too distant past and
in the present of many of us still, sex has been infused
with expectations, projections, anxieties and discomfort,
and the intimate sharing of sexual feelings has been discour-
aged by negative and highly repressive societal attitudes.
Nevertheless, has our more recent, proudly displayed
freedom in sexual encounters really helped connect us
with others, or is it simply just another expression of our
anxieties and unfulfilled needs in the form of thrashing
about against the outside flesh of others?

In such impersonal sexual activity there is little or no talk
of love, intimacy, trust, tenderness or vulnerability, a situation which can create deep psychological fragmentation.
Instead, sex is substituted for love and deep, committed
caring. It is staggering testimony to the powerful impact of
our culture, reflected in much of our films, theater, music
and advertising, that although there is not one among us
who has not felt unsatisfied, alone and abandoned after a
sexual encounter, we keep reaching out for others in the
plaintive hope that the next person will move us beyond
the steely casings of our own flesh and our aloneness.

Trained in shame and embarrassment, having lived our

lives with tremendous constraints upon our sexual behavior and confused about the nature of our sexuality, many of us fall into uneasy silence when it comes to discussing sexual matters with our children. And with our silence we guarantee that another generation will share our awkwardness and failure to achieve a deep and caring intimacy with loved ones.

Added to the awkwardness and non-communication that surround the issues of sexuality and intimacy in our families is the matter of sexual violence. For sexual violence takes place not only in families in which incestuous assault occurs but, to some degree and in some manner, in all of our homes. There are many forms this violence may take, including the perpetuation of our culture's personally debilitating, negative sexual attitudes, from which few if any of us have escaped. Because of a puritan tradition which grounds us in guilt and unrealistic role expectations, most of us remain confused about our sexuality and may perpetuate damaging sexual attitudes in our families.

Negative attitudes about sexuality fostered within a family can create a climate of such repression and denial of sexual feelings that even a child's innocent question about body function or casual exploration of his or her genitals can lead to overreaction on the part of other family members. The natural curiosity of children, their desire to touch and fondle themselves and their questions can cause families to exercise the ultimate sexual violence upon them: the denial of their right to their own bodies—the right to learn about them, to touch and enjoy them, to share them when they choose and to live wholly and delightedly within them.

We all have been guilty at one time or another of having violated or ignored our children's basic human rights. Many times children are unable to tell us what they experience precisely because they are considered to be our property and, as such, have no option in the family to be heard, particularly when they want to tell us things we do not want to hear. They know, for instance, what sort of touching is nurturing and what kinds are exploitive, but may not feel they have permission to tell us when grown-up family members touch them in ways that make them feel uncomfortable. We do not teach our children the freedom to express what they feel and know, and we often fail to respect their place among us. They are not seen, not believed and not heard, as the folk maxim has taught us.

Letting our children be who they are and reserving for ourselves our own fights, our own pasts and our own fears is a war that wages within us throughout our lives and the lives of our children. And for many of us, it is a war we lose too frequently. But not only do we lose, our children lose as well. Thus the seeds are planted for yet another generation of adults, filled with unmet needs, who will turn to others—either their marriage partners or children— to meet their needs for them.

So the circle is closed and we are caught within it. Those of us who are not battering parents, not physically or sexually abusive parents, are caught up in the same problem of relating to our children from a position of absolute power. Our abuse of our children may be more subtle, less dramatic; perhaps it doesn't come to the attention of authorities or counseling services. But we, too, damage our children whenever we fail to respect their human rights.

Incestuous assault, then, is only one of the more horrifying behaviors that result from the deadly situation in which children, who are powerless, are dominated by parents who turn to them for their own emotional, physical or sexual gratification.

In many cases, incestuous behavior serves as a process initiated by an adult to arrest the rate of disintegration that is occurring within the family. When a marital relationship becomes strained, when the roles and responsibilities of the adults in a family become blurred, when pain and estrangement grow to an extreme, there can occur among the family members an unconscious search for alternatives to that erosion. However, instead of turning toward the larger community in an effort to begin to identify and meet the emotional or sexual needs of its adult members, the incest family turns further inward upon itself to maintain the facade of a group of people who love and care for one another. The sexual incompatibility and misinformation, awkwardness and anxiety heighten not only the specific sexual tension between the estranged adults, but also increase the tension experienced by the family as a whole. If family members have not learned how to communicate their anxieties, the disintegration gathers its own momentum, and because there is no larger community with which the family is interacting that can help defuse some of its internal pressures, the self-contained, teetering nuclear unit has to try to absorb them all.

In such ingrown and dangerously powerless families in which adults cannot understand their own needs and how either to provide them for themselves or ask for them from their spouses, they may turn to their children for their survival. In this way, children are thrust forward into the roles left empty in the family system. In such families children sense, at a surprisingly early age, what is required of them to keep the family together, and they will do so, even at the price of their own victimization.

The family erosion which precipitates such role alterations can develop slowly or it can descend abruptly upon the family. For some men, decreasing status in the job market leading to a change in the family's social status can trigger long-buried doubts about their ability to provide and be successful in the limited definitions they were taught as young boys. For others, entering middle age can provoke anxiety about loss of youth, which may precipitate angry and vitriolic behavior directed at their families.

conspiracy of silence

In an effort to maintain their image as head of the household, these men may become increasingly tyrannical. Threats, physical violence and alcoholism often surface as the symptoms of their inner pain and alienation and, without recognition, will escalate as the men continue to find ways to mask their growing feelings of powerlessness and frustration.

When troubled families are isolated from the community in which they live, there is little opportunity for contact with whatever services might be available to provide effective intervention. A factor further discouraging aid to troubled families is that we tend to consider the nuclear family's isolation and self-imposed privacy to be a valuable source of strength. We believe that the family needs to be shielded and protected from the prying eyes of the larger community. Keeping family secrets from outsiders, teaching our children that "blood is thicker than water" and that outsiders are not to be trusted, we reinforce an unhealthy isolation of the nuclear family unit.

In themselves, sexual thoughts and feelings about members of our family are not uncommon, not unnatural; there is always a sensual component to our love relationships, particularly those with ones of our own flesh. However, such feelings can be acknowledged without being acted upon and can be understood in their naturalness if they are aired in the open. This is not the case in families whose members have not found ways to communicate openly with one another or with outsiders. Instead, adults who are unable to meet their own or each other's needs for warmth, nurturance and safety, and who may painfully remember their own feelings of powerlessness as children unable to defend themselves against abusing adults, inexorably precipitate abuse upon their offspring, resulting in generation upon generation of scarred and damaged children.

If no one interferes and no one intercedes, the incest family may continue for countless generations, without help and without change. Carrying within it the seeds of its own destruction and the crippling of its children, the family is trapped in not knowing and in not being able to reach beyond itself to the resources that can help its members better understand and alter their patterns of behavior.

The mother, father and child victim in such a family feel similarly abandoned, betrayed, isolated and needy. Neither parent has been able to satisfy his or her own or their child's needs for warmth, closeness and nurturing, and the child seeks comfort in whatever form it is offered.

The child's need for love becomes the precise source of his or her vulnerability. If the father begins to place upsetting and inappropriate sexual demands on the child, he or she often is not emotionally capable of exercising restraint and may be unable to turn to the mother for the love that is being expressed by the father in such distorted and frightening ways. In acquiescing, the child is displaying an adaptive response to the environment in the only way he or she feels is available. The child feels incapable of putting an end to the father's advances and feels abandoned and betrayed by the mother, who has not proven capable of protecting her offspring.

The father, unable to protect his child from his instincts or impulses, uses his position of authority to insist that such behavior is not wrong or inappropriate, and if the child is young enough, he or she most likely will believe him. The father avoids his guilt and responsibility by creating elaborate rationalizations—either his child is seductive or enjoys it, or he was just showing the child the facts of life. In any case, he makes a powerful attempt to deny his responsibility, and his behavior may become compulsive. By the time his child reaches adolescence, the father may become even more tyrannical and may insist on discouraging his or her social life. Thus, staggering under the weight of his own complicity, the father forces the family into a tighter and tighter ingrown group.

conspiracy of silence

The mother of an incest victim does not have cultural permission to express the fury and disappointment which remain smoldering inside her. Often, as her husband becomes more domineering, suspicious and possessive of their child, the mother retreats into an increasingly passive stance in the hope that it will ward off further quarreling. She is unable to protect either herself or her child, and her socialization as a woman in overvaluing men and devaluing herself traps her in conflicting and often masochistic behavior patterns.

Both parents know on a deeper level that they have failed to protect their child. Often witnesses or participants to abusive relationships as children, their own feelings of overwhelming helplessness make it difficult for them to play an active role in protecting their child. It is as though they identify with their child from past experience and painfully conclude that the abuse is as inescapable for their offspring as it was for them. Those who are unable to confront the reality of such a horrifying repeat performance refuse to admit that the abuse is happening. If the abuse is not acknowledged, if the denial and silence are firm enough, they can make themselves believe that it does not exist. And if it does not exist, then there is no need to deal with the pain of the child, both the one that lives unresolved within them and the one they did not protect.

Keeping silent about the abuse, virtually denying its existence, is the only way such a family believes it can remain intact. It is the vehemence of that silence that is so impacting to all family members, for it forces them to believe that what is happening is so terrible that it cannot be spoken aloud. To paraphrase R. D. Laing: incest families hide the truth of their lives to keep people in the dark about what is going on and in the dark that they are in the dark.

The world is changing so quickly and our values are altering so rapidly that perhaps the only lessons we have for

the family

our children are the truths about our own lives—whatever those truths are—for that is all we know. Part of the intimacy that could exist within the American family consists of a real sharing of our feelings, our fears, our uncertainties and our ambivalences, for that is the only way children can learn to accept and deal with similar feelings they may have experienced. It is when we withhold our true selves from our partners and our children that we are unable to form a real family. Instead, we live together as a group of painfully isolated individuals who simply share a surname.

THE PROFESSIONAL FAMILY

◆◆◆◆◆◆◆◆◆◆◆◆◆◆◆◆◆◆

Margaret

Silence and denial are not exclusively the responses of victims and their families in dealing with incestuous assault. The same responses are exhibited by many professionals who have been mandated to deal with damaged families. All too frequently, community service systems created to protect and serve children and their families intimidate, harass and further traumatize those they are supposed to help.

Following is one of the more extreme examples of a community's inept response to an incestuous assault case. The situation involved a mother and her four children, who had been sexually abused by their biological father. The mother's requests for help began when she discovered that her oldest child, a girl then five years old, was being molested by her husband. The father was, and probably still is, a leading political figure in the medium-sized midwestern city in which the family resides, and the mother is well known for her participation in civic and church activities.

the professional family

My contact with the case began when the mother tele-phoned a crisis center I was visiting. She had seen a poster which told of the frequency of incestuous assault and its prevalence among families of all economic groups. Appar-ently made bold by such a clear public statement of the problem she had grown to consider her private nightmare, the woman called the number given on the poster. The counselor who took her call remembered, "She talked like she was numb." And talk she did, for two hours, pouring out the history of her efforts to find help as well as her feelings of rage and impotence.

The following account of the woman's struggle to obtain help for her family is based on her conversations with the hotline counselor.

When Margaret's daughter, now twenty-six, was five years old, Margaret began to suspect something was going on—something her daughter did not have words to tell her about. The playing and fondling between the child and her father had changed subtly into a disquieting kind of inter-play. When Margaret confronted her husband, Ted, with her discomfort, he told her she must be "crazy" to be up-set about their activities. "All I was doing was stroking and playing with my daughter," he said, "like any good father."

Still feeling concerned, Margaret spoke with her husband's sister, a good friend who lived nearby. The sister assured her there was no need to worry about it, that it was "no big thing." She told Margaret that, in their family at least, such behavior was "natural" and went on to state that when she, her younger sister and Ted were young, and until Ted had passed through adolescence, they all had had sexual contact with each other. That was "just the way it was" in their family. Margaret was completely unable to accept this information and its implications for her own life. She spent days and nights thinking about it and be-came more and more upset.

conspiracy of silence

Preoccupied and distraught by turns, Margaret appeared noticeably agitated to her husband. He began watching her closely, commenting on her "strange behavior," and repeatedly asked her why she was "carrying on" as she was. This, coupled with her sister-in-law's repeated assurances that nothing out of the ordinary was going on, led her to doubt her own sense of the situation's reality. Within weeks Margaret was hospitalized with an emotional reaction that was thereafter referred to as her "nervous breakdown." The six weeks she spent in the hospital stigmatized her within her own and her husband's families as a woman who had been "sick" and whose word was therefore suspect.

The couple's oldest son, now twenty-one and in the army, was forcibly raped by his father at fourteen while the two were on a camping trip together. A neighboring camper witnessed the assault and reported it to the campground authorities, who assured him that such things "go on all the time" and for him not to get "so worked up about it."

The boy told his mother what had happened when he and his father returned from the camping trip, and Margaret went to an attorney in a nearby town for advice. The attorney, visibly shaken, suggested that an agreement be drawn up so that Ted would financially provide for the boy until he came of age. In effect, the boy was paid to go away and be quiet, which he did.

The other children in Margaret's and Ted's family are boy and girl twins, now twelve years old. During a recent vacation to the East Coast, the family visited Ted's youngest aunt. One night while Margaret was in an upstairs room changing for dinner, she heard her husband and daughter in the aunt's living room. Throwing on a robe, she hurried downstairs to find her husband adjusting his clothing and her daughter barricaded in the bathroom.

Margaret went to her husband's aunt and uncle and emotionally shared her fears about what was going on in their

146

*home, and the couple responded as calmly and indiffer-
ently as Ted's sister had. They insisted that Margaret was
"overreacting," that she seemed unable to discuss what
was happening "like a civilized person." Margaret's confidence in her own feelings and response to the abuse began
to waver in the face of two composed, level-headed adults
who were obviously quite relaxed about the situation.*

*After they returned home from their trip, Margaret
arranged to meet with the principal and assistant principal
of her children's school. She told them of the incestuous
abuse in her home and asked for their help and intervention with her children.*

*The administrators carefully explained that they did not
have counselors on staff who were trained in "that sort of
thing" but assured her they would do their best if her children came to them and requested counseling. The administrators' ability to deal with "that sort of thing" was never
tested. The children did not make any requests.*

*With the dwindling courage she had left, Margaret finally
approached the law. She went to the chief of police and
again related her reasons for concern, then asked what she
could do. The chief's response was brusque and final: "Get
yourself a gun and blow the bastard away if he ever comes
close to your kids again." Margaret gathered her purse and
gloves, thanked the chief and left.*

*The only place to which Margaret had not turned for
comfort and understanding direction was her personal
source of solace and refuge. The shame of her disclosure
would have to be borne one last time; she would go to her
church. Resolute, she attended the next meeting of the
church deacons. After church business had been discussed,
the meeting was opened to comments from the floor. At
that point Margaret stood up, was recognized and began a
public declaration of her desperation.*

*The people around her—people whom she had known,
worked and worshipped with even before she was married—*

first expressed openness, then horror and disbelief, and finally masked their feelings behind expressionless faces. Margaret finished by asking for suggestions from anyone present as to what else she might try to do. She was answered by a muffled cough or two, the sound of bodies moving uncomfortably about on wooden chairs and nothing else.

The next day Margaret was visited by two of the church trustees. They told her that the church board had met that morning and had decided unanimously to recommend that she not attend any further church functions until she had things "straightened out at home." Two days later she received a formal letter from the church reiterating the board's decision.

Currently Ted is continuing his long-term sexual relationship with his youngest daughter and is molesting his youngest son. The daughter appears quite ambivalent about the relationship, vacillating between outbursts to her mother that "everything is terrible," that she is unhappy and "doesn't know what to do to make it stop," and long periods when she reacts passively to her father's sexual demands. Margaret is sarcastically accused by Ted of being "sick" and "nuts." Margaret's oldest daughter, though married and with a family of her own, still is not free of the pattern that began when she was five. Casual visits from her father apparently still result in rape.

While he was growing up, Ted had been involved in a series of intrafamilial, consensual sexual relationships. Everybody had had sexual experiences with everyone else, and no one talked about it outside the family. Margaret's training had been traditional, with a strong church orientation. She and thousands of women like her have had nothing in their early lives to prepare them for anything other than highly conventional sexual relationships and certainly nothing to prepare them for the possibility that their spouses would sexually assault their children.

the professional family

Having received no help from within her family, Margaret turned to the larger community—the church, the school system, the police department and a lawyer—for guidance and understanding. She was met with silence, avoidance and a tacit condoning of the abuse at various levels of the community. Although Margaret's situation is extreme, it is not an uncommon experience; for there is a lack of effective family intervention services in nearly all of our communities.

Many men and women in the helping professions have been in a position to aid young victims of incestuous assault. School teachers, guidance counselors, social workers, pediatricians, family doctors, health workers and others have had reasons to suspect or know of incestuous abuse. In most cases, however, professionals have not felt adequately trained or experienced in handling sexual problems to deal with the abuse, to provide the care and intervention young victims need. Furthermore, most professionals still exhibit judgmental attitudes and discomfort when confronted with the sexual abuse of children within the family.

In the following case, Ingrid's experiences with both the medical and educational communities reflect the inadequate response to incestuous assault frequently encountered in the professional community.

Ingrid

Ingrid is a closed and guarded woman of fourteen years. Her adult status has not evolved naturally; rather, maturity was thrust upon her through a series of jolting experiences that spanned the first few months following her thirteenth birthday. Her young eyes reflect the bitterness of betrayal—betrayal by a father who sexually abused her and betrayal by a social system that repeatedly failed to support and defend her.

Ingrid's parents have been married for eighteen years, and Ingrid has two younger sisters. The first opportunity for agency intervention in the problems of Ingrid and her family came about when Ingrid reported to her junior high school's public health nurse. According to medical records, the girl complained of a burning sensation during urination. The school doctor's examination indicated a bladder infection and venereal disease.

The nurse's reaction was one of shocked disgust. First she soundly berated Ingrid for loose sexual conduct, then called the girl's mother to report the doctor's findings.

Ingrid's mother recalled her reaction to that telephone conversation:

"Imagine—a thirteen-year-old having a disease like that! I simply couldn't believe it. I kept asking the nurse whether there couldn't be some kind of mistake. That is the sort of thing that happens to kids from bad homes, kids who don't have parents to supervise them properly. I just couldn't seem to get it through my head that she was talking about my Ingrid. I suppose I must have overreacted, looking back on it. But there is no way to describe how I felt. It was just out of the blue. The idea that anybody knew about it, even a nurse, was almost as bad as Ingrid having the disease itself. Embarrassed isn't a strong enough word for what I felt. I finally told her to send Ingrid right home, and I just sat looking out on the street waiting for her. My mind was a complete blank.

"When Ingrid got home, I lit into her. I didn't wait for her to say anything; I just lit right in. I knew better than to believe those old wives' tales about getting a disease from toilet seats. She had been with somebody, and I was going to sit there until I found out who had done that to her.

"It didn't take too long until she got mad at how I was

being, like an inquisitor, and she told me. I think that was why she finally told—because she was mad at me. That was some reason, wasn't it?"

Ingrid remembered that scene, too:

"I didn't want to have to tell her. I had kept it a secret all the time it was happening. There were lots of times I wanted to tell somebody, but I felt so ashamed. But I started to have this awful burning every time I had to go to the bathroom, and I got scared and told the nurse. Just about that part of it. But she got a really suspicious look on her face when I described it to her and asked me lots more questions—and it just came out.

"Once I had told the nurse and the doctor, then everybody wound up knowing about it. All kinds of people. And I got so scared and shaky inside I didn't know what to say to them.

"Telling them it was Daddy made me feel worst of all. I remember my mom crying, and we went to a big hospital. We sat outside in a corridor with lots of other people making noise. Some of them had real big cuts on their heads, and one man kept crying about his leg.

"We sat there for a long time, and my mother didn't say much to me. Finally a nurse came and said for me to follow her and for my mother to wait outside. She made me take my clothes off and asked me all sorts of questions, and then a doctor came in. He asked me some more questions—stuff about what Daddy did to me, how long Daddy had been doing it and when it started. I knew I was supposed to tell the truth, but some of it got all jumbled up in my mind and I wanted him to stop asking me. Finally he and the nurse got real quiet and just looked at each other in a funny way.

"The doctor said he was going to look at me 'down there,' and I had to get up on the table and put my feet in some metal braces that opened up my legs real wide. Then he put a big, cold thing inside me, and it hurt. I told him it hurt, but I couldn't even see his face, and he didn't stop when I asked. There were sheets over my knees, and the doctor and the nurse were behind the sheets and my knees, and I could only see the ceiling. They stayed there for a really long time talking to each other, and they didn't say anything to me. I just tried to lie as still as I could and tried to concentrate on the ceiling. When they got finished, they told me to get dressed and that I would have to talk to some more people.

"When I came back outside into the hallway, where my mother was, she was crying again and talking to a policeman. They stopped talking when I came over, and he said for me to come into another room. Then he asked me some more questions about my daddy, and my mother just kept crying the whole time. My mother cries a lot. It used to make me mad, but I just stopped paying attention to it. That's usually what I do when something makes me mad— I just don't pay attention, and the being mad starts to go away."

Ingrid's mother added her recollections of that night:

"I just sat in the hospital corridor in a state of shock while they examined Ingrid. They took her history and called our family doctor for records and asked me how I wanted to proceed. I told them I wanted to proceed backward to when it was still morning and none of this had happened. They wanted to know what I was going to do about my husband, and I said I didn't want to see him in the house when I got home. They asked me if I wanted him picked up, and I said yes.

"I didn't know who to think about first—me or Ingrid or my husband. It all just got to be too much, and all I could do was sit there. After a while, a policeman came over to me and said they had gone to my husband's place of business and taken him in, and they had some questions for me. I couldn't even talk to him. When they told me they had picked him up, I realized that everybody would find out what had happened. I could never hold my head up anyplace I went. I had this feeling that people would be laughing at me and pointing their fingers.

"By the time Ingrid came out of the examining room, I was hysterical. They said they were going to take her to juvenile hall for a while, until they could sort out the facts. That's just what they called it—sorting out the facts. Like my life was something they could put down on a chart and list like a geometry problem or something. Ingrid hardly looked at me when the policeman told her they were taking her to a shelter, and another policeman said he was taking me to the station to fill out a complaint so they could hold my husband."

And, finally, Ingrid's father contributed still another dimension to the family's recollection of that day:

"I guess I knew it would come out sooner or later. God knows what I did wasn't right, but I never hurt her. I swear to that. I never hurt her.

"As soon as I saw them come in—the police, I mean—I knew just what was up. We drove to the local precinct, and they asked me all sorts of questions about when it started and how often I did it and things like that. They didn't want to hear my side of it. Every time I would try to explain how my wife drove me to it with her coldness and her always crying, they just didn't want to listen. They already had decided I was the guilty one and that was all there was to it.

"They brought my wife in, and she took one look at me and started that damn crying again. Hysterical women are something I cannot stand, and she is a classic case. She said she never wanted to see me again and didn't care if I spent my whole life in jail. They took her in another room, and I went to jail. Right then and there."

The results of that night's trauma for Ingrid and her family are consistent with most discovered cases of incestuous assault. Once the community's helping agencies—such as the school nurse, the hospital staff and the police—made a great uproar of outraged morality, they ceased efforts to provide support for the victim. Ingrid's father never came to trial. Although there was no doubt of his having sexually abused his daughter, neither Ingrid nor her mother would press charges.

A police officer in Colorado told me that well over eighty percent of the open-and-shut incestuous assault cases she investigated never came to trial. "The price is just too high," she explained. "Don't forget that the mother has a great need to prove to herself or to her family or to the neighbors that she wasn't a bad parent. In order to do that, often she will at least partially blame the child for letting it go on without telling. Of course, a great deal depends on the age of the child, the economic circumstances of the family and the relationship between husband and wife. But, for the most part, in my experience, incest cases just never come to trial. Without anyone to bring charges, our hands are tied.

"It's true that families bring considerable pressure to bear on the victim not to testify. If a young person does take the stand and is able to relate the specific nature of the sexual abuse, the child or the mother may oppose a guilty verdict that would send the offender to prison. In most incest cases, the offender's behavior probably continued over a period of years before it came to light. This fact, coupled with adult family ambivalence about prosecution, can greatly damage the credibility of child witnesses and leave them feeling confused, embarrassed and, again, alone and guilty."

Ingrid was sent to juvenile hall, where she is awaiting placement in an institution or foster home. She is older than the usual placement, and it is difficult to find homes for older children. Even more difficult, Ingrid now has a psychological and sexual history that could be frightening or upsetting to those families that might otherwise be prepared to care for a girl her age. Ingrid feels that being taken out of her home was punishment for what she did. Her guilt is sealed in silence and withdrawal.

The first public recognition of Ingrid's problem took place at her school. Logically, that was the point at which sensitive intervention might have been offered to her. Why wasn't it?

We assume we have provided for our schoolchildren's needs: we hire visiting nurses to be sure students are in good health, require immunizations to be certain children are protected from serious diseases and pay for hot-lunch programs and staffs of guidance counselors. Teachers hold periodic parent conferences, formulate careful lesson plans and maintain tidy records of students' attendance, citizenship and scholastic achievements.

Indeed, we like to think we are caring for the whole child. However, seldom do any of our educational efforts speak to the issue of sexually victimized children. There are special sex-education classes in schools to deal with the biological facts of reproduction but not the more complex nature of sexuality—nothing that speaks to the feelings or anxieties our children experience concerning their bodies and sexual responses. Educators are as uncomfortable with such matters as is the rest of society, so that the more emotionally awkward issues of sexual ethics and morality— rather than stern lectures about venereal disease as a consequence of sexual activity—seldom are openly discussed. As a result of this educational void, children are left to share a wealth of misinformation with each other or remain uninformed.

In school, to whom can children go for advice and support concerning sexual abuse, ignorance or anxiety? Are children to be held accountable for keeping sexual secrets when the adults in our schools have made it clear that they do not want to hear about them?

conspiracy of silence

Not all victims remain silent, however. Some, finding the burden of their secret exploding within them, begin to behave in ways educators see as bad: their grades plummet; they become aggressive toward other children; they express their pain in as many individual ways as there are children. And often they are punished for doing so.

In sexual abuse cases involving children, schools can do very little—at least at the present time. A nurse responding with openness and compassion to Ingrid's situation might have spared her the trauma she experienced during her medical examination; a counselor might have been able to arrange a meeting with Ingrid and her mother to determine what course of action and alternatives they could have pursued together; a teacher might have gone to the hospital with Ingrid and her mother. But there are too few individuals within the school system who are comfortable with such matters, too few who are skilled in providing alternative solutions and too few who want to become involved.

What about the medical people who handled Ingrid's case? We expect our doctors and nurses to be trained and sophisticated in treating all kinds of people for all sorts of ailments. We would like to think of them as a resource for young victims of incestuous assault. The image of a kindly, wise, unhurried doctor who is unflappable in any situation is one that many of us carry in the face of experiences that should have taught us better.

For Ingrid and most other sexual abuse victims, the hospital services presently available fall far short of providing the supportive, non-threatening atmosphere vital to a victim's emotional needs. There are many reasons for this lack of emotional support.

Dr. Suzanne Sgroi, a physician and project internist for Connecticut's Child Abuse and Neglect Demonstration Center, explained some of the reasons in an article

the professional family

published in 1975: "In medical parlance, child molestation is the least popular diagnosis. . . . It seems to be 'too dirty,' 'too Freudian' or perhaps 'too close to home.' Thus, one who becomes concerned with this particular aspect of child protection must be prepared to cope with a very high degree of resistance, innuendo and even harassment from some, as well as indifference from others. The pressure from one's peer group, as well as the community, to ignore, minimize or cover up the situation, may be extreme."[1]

This view is confirmed by Dr. Ray Helfer, a pioneer in the field of child abuse. Although his work focuses primarily on the physical battering of children, he believes many of the same factors account for why physicians and pediatricians are not involving themselves in matters concerning either sexual or physical abuse within the family: "The first reason [for non-involvement] is that we haven't been trained to deal with the problem. . . . We were not taught it in our medical schools; we were not taught the interpersonal skills that are necessary to deal with families we don't like . . . [and] it's very easy not to like parents who beat up or neglect [or sexually misuse] their kids."[2]

In addition to this lack of training, Helfer points out the lack of interdisciplinary approaches necessary to deal with the rising number of reported cases: " . . . we do not learn how to work with members of other disciplines or other professions, as peers. For at least ten years, from the end of our undergraduate years through medical school, internship and residency, we deal only with physicians; we may encounter a few professionals, but not, for the most part, as peers. Consequently, sitting around a table with a lawyer, a social worker, a policeman, a judge, the court workers and department of social services workers . . . all of whom have equal, and some greater, authority in these cases than we do . . . is very threatening."[3]

It is indeed threatening. And very close to home. Most treatment patterns, when they exist at all, still are patterned after the medical model, with the standard operating procedure one of diagnosis, labeling and either prosecution of the offender or, in cases in which prosecution is impossible, a recommendation that the child be removed from the home.

And, as Dr. Sgroi puts it, "Recognition of sexual molestation of a child is entirely dependent on the observing individual's inherent willingness to entertain the possibility that the condition may exist."[4]

Parents, professionals, teachers, adults in general cannot believe these children because they do not want to believe them. To acknowledge the truth of what victims are trying to tell us forces us to re-examine too many cherished beliefs—beliefs about the absence of childhood sexuality, beliefs about the protection significant adults in a child's life are supposed to provide and, most important, beliefs about a society in which such things can happen. It is easier for us to sweep truth under the rug of our traditional assumptions, because to face truth squarely is too risky and dangerous.

Even when child victims are believed, there are few clearly delineated, systematic procedures that have been developed to deal with the medical, emotional and psychological needs of the victims. There are few legal precedents endorsing court-supervised treatment of sex offenders in the community as an alternative to prosecution and incarceration. There are few services available to provide wholistic counseling to victims and their families.

At best, what we now have is a multitude of self-regulating agencies, public and private, without a comprehensive plan for effective, constructive family intervention. Few communities employ a team approach to the multiple problems of a sexually abusive or exploitive family, which compounds the confusion, encourages more traumatization and results in irresolute and limited agency activity.

The criminal justice system is set up to identify, apprehend and punish those members of society who break society's laws. It is not in the business of understanding the reasons those laws may have been broken or exploring alternative ways of rehabilitating offenders. The courts have been mandated to punish.

If an incestuous assault case is reported, a police officer may be the first representative of the criminal justice system to contact the family. The officer usually is a man and frequently has children of his own. Often, horrified and appalled at contact with a sex offender, he may feel as many police officers I have met have stated—that all they want to do to such men is "cut off their balls."

Like the system they serve, such men's energies usually are centered upon apprehension and punishment of offenders, with minimal thought for the problems of victims. With a sex crime, law enforcement personnel usually are under pressure from an outraged community and must develop a sure-fire case against the offender. Such a narrow focus leaves little room for concern about the ongoing trauma of the young victim and the emotional pain he or she suffers.

Involvement in the incestuous relationship is difficult enough for a child victim. When the incest is reported to the police and the young person is subjected to repeated questioning about each painful detail by a barrage of uniformed strangers, shame and embarrassment can magnify the situation out of all manageable proportion.

If the offender is arrested, the nightmare of testifying at the arraignment or preliminary hearing is added to the ordeal of police interrogation. If the crime is a felony, the child also must appear before a grand jury to give testimony. After the indictment comes the actual trial. In most jurisdictions, trial is held in an adult criminal court, and much too often it is a jury trial conducted in an open court. The full gamut of pretrial appearances, testifying and cross-examination can be especially traumatizing to the child. Efforts by defense counsel to discredit or confuse the child witness, even when held to a minimum, can be a terrifying ordeal for the victim.

When incestuous offenders are prosecuted, child victims must undergo the same procedures as adult victims; seldom are any special procedures or protection provided. Protocols have been developed for juvenile offenders in the criminal justice system but not for juvenile victims. These children are caught up in a system too complex, too threatening and too overwhelming for them to understand.

Not only do legal proceedings further traumatize a child victim, but the prosecution often is ultimately unsuccessful because the child is unable or unwilling to provide the clear and unshakeable statements necessary for conviction. The victim is expected to remember and recount, in graphic detail, a sexual relationship that may have been going on over a considerable period of time. Dates, places, descriptions of acts and frequency are vital in prosecuting an adult, but such information can be difficult for the child to reconstruct.

The following passage indicates some of the difficulty involved in interviewing child witnesses:

> Knowledge of the basic principles of child development has immediate significance for law enforcement personnel when investigating sexual abuse cases. Obviously the child cannot be a witness unless s/he has acquired verbal skills. In the case of the pre-verbal child who has been molested, another witness or corroborating evidence would be necessary in pursuing prosecution.
>
> Although children develop the beginnings of verbal language between the ages of two and four years, concepts, metaphor, connections between events, causality, are not present.
>
> The older child, four through six, often has difficulty reconstructing in a logical and orderly fashion

the ideas of time, space and distance as might relate to the assault.

Children through the age of ten have some difficulty differentiating between fact and fantasy. Though the young person may be able to distinguish between the two realities, a fantasy projection that extricates them from a painful or difficult emotional situation may be utilized.

The school-age child, six through eleven, is better prepared to respond to the expectations of an interviewer . . . as they are beginning the gradual shift from total reliance on family to a peer culture.[5]

Rebecca, an incest victim who now facilitates a group for other victims, flatly states: "In all my experience with victims, never once have I known one to lie about the assault having taken place. In fact, it most often is the opposite. Kids will lie to convince people that it didn't happen, just to protect their family."

It is difficult for a prosecutor to establish the credibility of a child victim in an incestuous assault case. Adults are extremely reluctant to believe a child over an adult because they fear that children will make up stories in anger to punish parents for imagined wrongs. The responsibility rests solely upon the police and prosecutor to evaluate the child's testimony, since seldom is there corroborating testimony.

Therefore child victims are required to prove themselves to those in authority. They must reassure adults that they are telling what may be the most painful truth of their young lives. Often a child doesn't want to tell at all, and that reluctance is seen as proof that the child is lying—a classic example of double-bind. For many young female victims, the reality of an almost totally male-dominated courtroom situation can be further upsetting, making it more difficult for them to say the awkward and painful things the court is waiting to hear.

An experienced social worker paints the grim court picture quite succinctly:

> Society, through its system of administering justice, requires that a person charged with an offense has a right to trial and to confront and cross-examine those who have brought the charges.
>
> What does harm to the victim is our society's need to have them repeat the details of the offense several times, to police, prosecutors and to the jury, sometimes with the assaulter present.
>
> What perhaps in the child's mind is a short-lived traumatic event with no permanent consequences thus is placed out of proportion to its importance, and forces the child to reorientate his or her ideas toward an adult interpretation of the offense and the child's own role in punishing the offender.
>
> Most police and prosecutors have had no training in nondamaging methods of interviewing children, and tend to use adversary approaches more appropriate for adults. The offender's lawyer has the duty of defending the client with every possible tool, and in so doing, may contribute to or inflict emotional damage on the victim by attempting to show that the victim is incompetent, seductive, malicious, a "Lolita," or has brought false charges.
>
> The dilemma here is the need to protect the child from the potential trauma of legal proceedings, but at the same time to convict and rehabilitate the offender. This dilemma can be somewhat reduced by using special interrogation. Even so, many parents may refuse to bring in the legal authorities for fear of reputational damage to the child and family. If courts cannot eliminate the trauma of testifying, nonreporting may be the best choice.[6]

the professional family

With incestuous assault, non-reporting is the choice most often made. The price is simply too high. The child's ambivalence about testifying, the pressure placed on the child not to testify by others in the family who want to protect their reputation, the child's credibility as a witness in the eyes of the legal system, the child's inexperience with legal jargon, the need for endlessly repeated testimony and the presence of the sexual offender, often shackled, in the courtroom are reasons that prosecutions seldom make it through the court system to trial and sentencing.

When the offense cannot be proven in court, or the victim will not testify, the community turns away from the child and his or her family, leaving them to try and reconstruct their lives with fewer resources than they had before society intruded. The victim's suffering continues. The child has been identified publicly with the incestuous relationship and must re-enter what he or she then sees as a hostile family environment, unprotected. If the sexual aggressor remains within the family, punishment of the child can be subtle, in the form of extra chores or restricted freedom. In some cases, punishment takes the form of violent repetition of the original abuse.

Sadly, family agency personnel usually handle incestuous assault cases poorly or in a damaging manner in coordinating their efforts with other agencies whose services the victims and their families need. Presumably it is the child who has been victimized and should be afforded primary care and concern. Whether or not that occurs depends upon many variables. Our police, physicians, social workers and teachers are no different from the rest of us. They, too, can be given to making cultural and social assumptions about incest victims.

It is easy and natural to feel outrage at the sight of ten-year-old girls or boys who have been sexually molested. Their tender years, their complete vulnerability and their

163

powerlessness engender protective sympathy for them and our self-righteous indignation at their parents.

But what of the young victim who is a hostile, sexually active, well-developed fourteen-year-old? Or a teenager who has become involved with drug or alcohol dependency, or has been truant from school or has repeatedly run away and perhaps prostituted him/herself to survive on the streets of an unfamiliar city? Our outrage and protectiveness aren't manifested quite as readily then, and courts do not see such victims as totally credible. Instead, it is assumed that if the incestuous abuse occurred over a period of years, the victim must have been either encouraging or a willing party to the abuse. Furthermore, the victim's response to the abuse, if it assumes the form of socially or sexually inappropriate behavior, may lock professionals more firmly into their biases and assumptions about the morality of the victim and the degree of the victim's responsibility for the sexual intrusion.

Adolescent victims often are confused and frightened, not only by the inappropriate sexual relationship but also about society's reaction upon discovering the relationship. Without sensitive and skillful handling, the medical examination, police intervention in the home and subsequent legal procedures can prove to be additional sources of trauma for them. Careless handling of a case coupled with the victim's feelings of guilt and embarrassment can greatly exacerbate the damage already done to the child.

The victim's feelings also are acutely influenced by the response of the family to the assault. As hard as it is to tell someone outside the family of his or her father's sexual assaults, the child's ambivalence often is compounded by the response of the mother to agency intervention. If the victim's mother is angry, either at the child or the aggressor, if she is distrustful of the child's accusations, if she becomes panicked and fearful, the child is left in a position of emotional isolation. There is no one to provide the support and encouragement he or she needs to face the frightening problem. Furthermore, if the parent's horror or denial is mirrored by the child-protection service personnel with whom the family has first contact, the similarity of response heightens the victim's sense of having "caused all that trouble," fear of being punished and shame at having his or her family condemned by others so caught up in their own visceral responses to the abuse that they are unable to respond in a caring and helpful way to the child's emotional needs.

When a non-involved third party suspects that sexual abuse is occurring in a home and wants to ensure the safety of a child, he or she may call a child-protection agency to request intervention. Most often the agency responds with a perfunctory phone call to the reported family requesting permission to make a home visit. Even if this request is granted, the entire family often denies to the visiting worker that anything untoward is going on. When there are no other obvious signs of abuse or neglect, such as visible bruises on the child's body, alcohol or chemical dependency of the parents, a sudden drop in the child's school grades or a record of abrupt behavior changes in the child, the worker shrugs, returns to the agency and closes the case. And whoever had the courage to report his or her suspicions in the first place probably won't have the heart to try again.

Even in the rare situation when a child victim is strong enough to say, and keep on saying, that sexual abuse is going on—to speak out in the face of the family's power structure, to keep saying it when his or her parents and other adults try to deny the truth by saying the victim is "making it up" or "has always been a bad kid" or "is just trying to get back at us because we punish him/her about school grades"—if, when all the odds are against it, someone, anyone, believes the young person's statements, what happens?

The patterns begin again. Almost without exception, no matter what action society takes, the victim is further victimized.

If a social service worker is assigned to the home and determines that the family is critically dysfunctional in major aspects of its interrelationships, or that there are strong indications of physical and emotional neglect, then the child will be removed from the home. But even with all the bad environment that may have contributed to the decision to place the child in a shelter, the child is taken from the only home he or she has had and is isolated from the only group of people he or she has known. Without careful counseling, the child will interpret being removed as punishment and abandonment.

There are occasions when children need to be removed from their homes for their own protection. Before such a decision is made, however, several criteria need to be closely examined: how long the incest has gone on and the likelihood of reoccurrence, the emotional and physical health and stability of the victim's mother and her ability to provide a safe and nourishing home life for her child, and the potential for violence in the home, directed either at the victim or mother by the offending adult. Often the offender is so caught up in his own denial system, either insisting that the incestuous abuse never occurred or that someone else was responsible for it, that there is little likelihood the abuse will stop if the family is left on its own to correct and reconstruct itself.

When a member of the family is willing to press and maintain charges, the aggressor is removed from the home, arrested and, if convicted as a sex offender, sent to prison. There he may be given aversion and drug therapy as part of the "treatment" our civilized society has devised for "sick minds." If these men had problems before they entered prison and then are forced to live in an all-male, confined situation for a number of years, what will they be like when they return to our streets and our communities?

Many in the criminal justice field believe that incarceration is an important part of therapy because it satisfies the aggressor's deep need to be punished and thus helps expiate his guilt. Such traditionalists feel the offender may punish himself in other ways if the criminal justice system does not do it for him.

There is, however, a growing body of legal and mental health professionals who do not agree with traditional theory. They maintain that the original sexual assault is brought on, in great part, by the offender's feeling of isolation and estrangement from adult society. Most sex offenders seem unable to initiate or maintain rewarding emotional and physical relationships at a peer level, so they turn to less threatening and relatively powerless children for sexual comfort and release of tension. The incestuous aggressor chooses a young family member, already physically available and emotionally accessible. Since feelings of isolation and estrangement are what precipitate an offender's behavior, forced isolation and estrangement for years in a penal institution can and do add to the offender's emotional wounds.

Incarceration of the aggressor does not seem to be the answer in most incestuous assault cases. What seems more appropriate is confinement of the offender in or near the family's community, along with a judicial mandate for the aggressor and all family members to enter therapy individually and as a group. Incestuous assault is a family situation, a family secret, a family problem. All family members are affected by the abuse, and all should be part of whatever rehabilitation efforts society can provide.

Most American families still consider their house of worship to be their ultimate source of comfort and guidance, the place where society's moral, ethical and spiritual guidelines are taught and the place to seek solace and direction, especially in times of crisis.

conspiracy of silence

That's how we think it should be. However, when I questioned the leaders of churches and temples across our country about sexual abuse problems within their congregations, they uniformly told me that they "don't see or hear much of that." When pressed, their explanation was something to the effect that they are not called upon in such situations. A few men of the cloth eventually acknowledged that they did hear such things in the privacy of their offices or in the confessional, but said they felt bound by their vows of silence and confidentiality to protect the anonymity of those who had shared their guilt and secrets in an effort to find help or absolution.

Most religions provide their followers with a person who serves as a sort of middle ground between them and their deity and who becomes a source of strength and wisdom for them in times of stress and crisis. Most religious leaders fulfill their responsibilities capably and in a truly dedicated fashion—except for dealing with uncomfortable sexual behavior problems.

Seminaries teach sexuality in its abstract forms—not in its aberrant manifestations. If our churches, temples and multi-denominational houses of worship continue to claim ignorance of sexually traumatic experiences and fail to be a resource in this area of family dysfunction, they will be knowingly denying the basic tenet of any ministry by turning away from the rawest, deepest kind of human need. Religious leaders can do more than tend to the spiritual needs of their congregations; they can be a powerful resource for helping their parishioners cope with the most basic pressures and tensions of their individual and family lives.

Incest victims and others who have been sexually traumatized should be able to obtain help from trained therapists who have resolved their own personal anxieties and sexual hangups. But it is difficult to find sensitive therapists who are both qualified and willing to work with sexually traumatized individuals without carrying their own anxieties and/or personal problems into their counseling.

There are significant exceptions to the experiences described in the following history, and effective, responsible treatment centers are being organized throughout our country at this very moment. The compassionate and skillful counseling resources presently available in our communities must be identified, embraced and fully utilized, and new resources must be developed. Our failure to do so may result in further distress for incest victims, as Estelle so clearly described to me.

Estelle

Estelle is a social worker trained in a variety of therapeutic techniques. In her opinion, the mental health community's view of early sexual trauma, and particularly incest, is badly distorted.

"I remember being in a class in my school of social work that was being taught by a renowned psychoanalyst whose writings I very much respected. He was talking about incest and the oedipal complex and telling the class that victims of incest were very disturbed because the acceptable fantasy of the oedipal complex became an unacceptable reality.

"That part seemed to make sense—that a little girl's loving desire for her father becomes confused and distorted if the father figure physically acts on the child's fantasized desire. Logically, such inappropriate action would affect the child's development in a most profound way.

"But then my hero went on to flatly state that people with actual incest experience develop an untreatable psychosis as a result of their experience. I was outraged and wanted to jump up and yell, 'You're a liar! *I'm* not psychotic.'

"What he said in that one sentence not only reinforced much of the inhibited conventional thinking about incest, but terribly accelerated my personal terror about my locked-up past. Part of the reason I'm so locked up is because the situation was so horrible, but the other part of my reason for denying my feelings is because I'm afraid those feelings are psychotic.

"When I began trying to find help, it was the beginning of a bitter education in human failings. As I went from therapist to therapist, it became terribly clear that the supposedly dispassionate professionals seemed just as titillated by my story of incestuous involvement with my father as my father had been excited by the actual experience with me.

"I became a wreck. I tried to kill myself. I was so depressed I didn't know if I could, or wanted to, survive in a world where fathers violated their little girls. So I went to a therapist who seemed strong and together and was the only person to whom I had been able to tell my terrible history. When my secret was out, he proceeded in ways he thought were best, to try to help me. One of the things he wanted to do was to help me unlock the history of my past. The way he went about that was to suggest I relate to him in a sexual way.

"At this time in my life I was fairly promiscuous, trying desperately to bury the relationship with my father under the bodies of whatever boys and men I could entice. I would end up attaching myself to males who would abuse me as my father had.

"In my work with the therapist, I remained blocked, and he suggested that I start talking to his penis. That developed into very specific sexual activities. I guess I was playing out my trip with my father in some fashion, but it still was uncomfortable to relate to someone I had come to for professional help in such an unprofessional manner.

"During my five years of treatment, we progressed from the traditional posture of me alone on the couch in a darkened room to me sitting alone in a chair. That was so

170

different from the darkened room and the lying down that we hurried on to the next step: lying down together on the carpeted floor. We'd lie there and hold hands, and I'd kiss him.

"What he did totally reinforced the neurotic patterns that had become habitual as a result of the relationship with my father. As my father had been, my therapist became. He was seductive to me sexually, he was loving and he insisted that *I* was the sick one. When I think back, it was a love relationship. We were lovers armed together against the terrible enemy within me.

"It's taken me years to undo the damage he did. Eventually I got myself together enough to realize he was not helping me, but I had become hopelessly dependent on him. It took me years to extricate myself from this dependency. When I told him I could no longer be dependent on him and he let me go, I was convinced I would never go to another therapist.

"About a year later, however, I went into one of the depressions that have been part and parcel of my existence ever since I was a child, and felt I needed help. I was fed up with traditional psychoanalytic therapy and thought I would see someone trained in more active techniques.

"I found another man with many credentials, began my visits and was delighted to discover he was not only well trained in traditional psychoanalytic techniques but was eclectic enough to blend in gestalt, psychosynthesis and Feldenkrais as well. Plus he was warm, seemed open and was willing to help me work my problems through. He was wonderful, until I developed the crush on him that's usual with the transference process.

"As with my former therapist, I reminded him of my heavy emotional burdens around sexuality and that I hoped he would proceed carefully. I really wanted him to be able to deal successfully with what was happening. He was warmly reassuring that all would continue to go well.

"In addition to my private sessions, I also was a part of a group he led, and during the course of treatment I became uncomfortably certain there was something sexual going on between him and one of the other women in the group. After one of our meetings had broken up, I finally asked him if what I suspected was true—that he was physically involved with the group member. He absolutely denied it.

"Weeks later, I went out for coffee with the woman and laughingly shared what I called my 'crazy suspicions.' Her response was immediate and shattering: 'You're not crazy— we're lovers,' she told me.

"All I could think of was how he had lied and, like my father, had let me think I was crazy. No matter where I went for help, they somehow managed to reinforce the terrible patterns of my childhood I was trying so hard to break.

"By this time in my therapy, I was into my second year of training for social work. Through a number of reading assignments and lectures—very conservative and thought-ful—I had been exposed to many cautions regarding a therapist's need to control a patient's counter-transference so the therapist did not project his own unresolved issues onto the patient.

"I went to my next scheduled session reinforced in my belief that my therapist had betrayed both my trust and his profession. He saw matters differently. My accusation that he had falsely declared an integrity he did not possess elicited a bland denial that this was the case. He main-tained adamantly that he was perfectly justified in his physical relationship with a patient, that he was one of the new breed of enlightened contemporary therapists who were not bound by the old rules of non-involvement. According to him, my ethics were outdated and inappro-priate, and that ended my last attempt to master my problems with the help of experts. Just plain everyday common sense would have worked better."

In this enlightened age, things cannot get much more depressing in terms of our social system's response to the sexually traumatized. Those of us who work in the helping professions must start where we are. We are people first of all, and we share with the rest of society certain biases, stereotypes and confusions about sexuality. Therefore, unless we work to lower our anxiety levels through a genuine knowledge of human sexuality and the consequences of sexual trauma, we may remain unable to provide non-judgmental, compassionate and truly therapeutic intervention for the sexually abused.

Each of us as professionals must look inside ourselves before we can hope to provide help and guidance for others. We are a nation of brilliant achievers. Let's acknowledge our ignorance in this area and begin together to create the kind of intervention that is so desperately needed.

HISTORY OF
A SURVIVOR

♦♦♦♦♦♦♦♦♦

Theresa has many reasons for wanting to tell her story, and I have many for wanting it to be told. She has struggled to come to terms with her past and understand it, and the price has been very high. Most importantly, she has survived.

   To become the person she is now—living in a bustling city with her husband and small child, working and studying to prepare herself for a future full of new dreams and plans—Theresa had to conquer nearly overwhelming forces of ignorance and denial that scarred her as she grew up. When telling me of her childhood, she often paused for long moments to order the painful memories that were surfacing. But Theresa has become a fiercely strong woman and permits herself no illusions, no hiding places. In forcing herself to bring the memories back, she gives us the courage to face similar remembered pain and to take responsibility for the hurt we have caused others in our own desperation. Only by facing the truths of the past can we surmount them and move, as she is moving, toward a future that is clear and honest. Those are my feelings. These are Theresa's.

"A child who is a victim of sexual abuse feels so terribly alone. If I could alleviate some of that, I would feel my time had not been wasted reliving the guilt and the aloneness.

"Recently I saw a television program where a young victim spoke of being put in the county jail because she 'knew too much to be put in juvenile with kids.' I didn't go through jail or anything, but I can really sympathize with what she meant. Once you realize how bad it is for kids to be involved with grown-up sex, until you really know how bad it is, you just don't think about it. But when someone finds out, and everybody tells you how evil it is, you feel so bad and worthless and different from everybody else.

"You are the *victim*—and that's what's so totally unfair and so totally wrong, that these people make you feel guilty. They pile all that guilt on you, and you're only a child. Just a kid.

"And I don't believe that all the people who do different kinds of sexual things with kids are all evil, nasty, terrible people. I think a lot of them are as much victims as I was. These people never grew, never learned. And there are thousands of these people today, and they need help as much as I ever did. I have to try to bring it out into the open and not feel ashamed about it anymore, even though everybody says you're supposed to be.

"I didn't have a childhood, no semblance of a childhood. I grew up too fast, too quick and all wrong. But here I am today. I'm lucky, I guess, to be where I am, and maybe I can hold out my hand to others who may not be there yet. That's what being a person is about, anyhow. Holding out your hand.

"It began when I was very small, and I think what was

really bad is that you don't know the difference. You haven't learned anything about right and wrong yet, so it's frustrating. Somehow you know something is wrong, but you can't quite put your finger on it. I never really had intercourse with any of them, but they were sexual acts nonetheless, and the effect on me was still the same.

"The first time I remember was with my first stepfather. There were a lot of stepfathers, but he was the first. He was a gross, fat person and I remember him telling me to do this thing to him, and I did it. It was not disgusting, the act itself, but *he* was disgusting because of his appearance. I didn't know what a father was supposed to do and not do, and I keep reminding myself that I was only four, only four. I spent a lot of years judging that four-year-old as I would have an adult before I finally realized I couldn't keep doing that—that it wasn't really fair.

"That first marriage was a short one, and he left pretty soon after he made me do that act on him. My mother married again shortly afterward, and he was a kind man. He took me on trips, and we went camping together. There were lots of good times. But, you see, my mother worked swing shift—she always worked—and she was never home when I went to bed. So he started to say things to me like, 'Come and get in bed with me and we'll stay warm together.' Well, things happened. Not vicious things, not hurtful things, but things nonetheless. And I think if I had never learned that they were wrong, I wouldn't have felt the horrendous guilt that came later. At the time, I didn't feel any guilt at all. I didn't know the difference. In my family, when a grownup said to do something, you did it. If a grownup had told me to go and stand on my head in the corner, well, I guess I would have.

"The years went by, and he and I got very close. They stayed married for only about five years, I guess, but to my mind it was a long time because they were such formative years for me.

history of a survivor

"I was raised as a Catholic, and by the time I was eight or nine years old I began to get the impression that something was fishy. In those days the church was very judgment-oriented, and as a child you felt—I felt—like a worm in the church because I was so low and God was so high and I was just about as worthless as a piece of sand. So trying to deal with the church and trying to deal with my home life was hard, because I couldn't even go up and say, 'Father, I think I'm doing something wrong, but I'm not sure. Is this right or wrong?' You couldn't go to a priest and say that. If there was a doubt in your mind if something was right or wrong, it was automatically wrong—that's the way I was raised. So I began to withhold this kind of information in the confessional, and to a Catholic girl the confessional is sacred. So this ended up building guilt on top of guilt.

"And then he died. He drowned. I watched him drown. He was about five hundred feet away from us, and I couldn't do anything. And afterward I felt guilty for that, that I hadn't jumped in the water and tried to save him. His nephew had drowned a year before, out of the same boat, and my stepfather had felt very guilty about this, and I suspect it was suicide. The wish was there and the opportunity presented itself.

"For almost a year after he drowned, my mother and I never talked about it. We never said anything because I didn't want to hurt her and she didn't want to hurt me. But after a year she and I went to a shrink. My school suggested it because I wouldn't talk, you know, and the shrink kept asking her things like, 'How was your childhood? What were your parents like?' And she told me when we left, 'I wouldn't tell him a damn thing. It's none of his business.' My mother was very proud like that. She wouldn't complain to strangers.

"After he died, it was nearly two years before she married again. I was almost glad then, although I loved him, that he had died, because at least I had my mom to myself for a while. But of course I couldn't tell anybody that, and it just made me feel even more awful and guilty.

"I was about ten or eleven by this time, and my mom left me alone most of the time, working and trying to keep things together, you know. My big sister had already left home by this time, and at night, when Mom was working, I would be by myself in this big, old flat with a big, long staircase inside, with the wind whistling up and down the stairs, and I would be terrified. Sometimes I would urinate on the living-room floor so I wouldn't have to go down the long hallway to the bathroom. I would try to rotate the spots on the floor so nobody would notice. And then she'd come home from work and everything would be okay again. She floated in and out of my life, but most of the time I was by myself.

"When she married again I was sort of glad because I thought we could finally be a family, all together. But this husband had cancer. He was dying even then and had only a year to live, the doctors said, but she loved him. He was the only one she ever really loved. All the rest were to help in the house, to bring in some money and keep her from being so lonesome. He was a college-educated man, a C.P.A., but he was the same.

"He used to use some kind of drug. I guess now it was for the pain of the cancer, but then I didn't know what it was, and he told me he'd hurt me if I told anybody he used it. It was a funny white powder, and it used to make him act awful with me. It wasn't actual sex, but it was everything else. He would tell me how soft and warm I was, and the opportunity was there since Mom was still working the swing shift. And even though I knew by now it was wrong, I couldn't tell. I didn't want to hurt my mother because I was sure she didn't know, and I couldn't tell at church, so I went along.

"It was very hard for me then—the judgment of the church on one side and on the other side the need to accept what kept happening as a reality I couldn't find a way to change. Finally I told my mother. I couldn't hold it in anymore. She was shocked and angry at him for having done those things to me, and she kicked him out right then.

"The next day I was coming home from school, really happy that day because he was going to be gone. I walked into the house and he had hung himself, right there in the kitchen. He was just hanging there. I walked over to a girl-friend's house and told her, and she called the police. And when they came, they made me go back upstairs and watch them while they cut him down.

"That was a scene I will never forget. They should have had some kind of delicacy, but I guess the law said they couldn't be in the house without somebody else there, so I had to watch. And then they let him lay there, and they didn't cover him up or anything else, and I had to go through all the questioning.

"After that, I didn't talk—*really* didn't talk—for almost six months because I stuttered so badly. People used to think I was retarded because of the stuttering. In school, too, they used to treat me like I was dumb, and they would laugh at me, which made it worse. I always had an awful terror of being laughed at, and there were times when I was in real despair.

"My mom had been paying money for me to have speech lessons in school, but after that happened and the stutter-ing got so bad, all the lessons went down the drain and I was right back where I started. Even worse.

"For a while she was so loving and protective, and I felt safe with her, and then she turned around and got involved with the same thing all over again. I was in the beginning of the eighth grade, and this man lived in another county. We moved up there for a while and I started a new school, but the same pattern started repeating itself again when-ever he and I were alone.

"Mother always kept working because even though she

married to get security for us, in the long run she never really got it. The strongest memory I have of my mother was at the ironing board. She worked for six days and on the seventh day she ironed. I always had to look right. She was always cleaning me and the house from top to bottom. She was very particular, and if I came home from school dirty I would end up in hot water, literally. I was a girl, and girls didn't get dirty. She hardly ever spanked me, and when she did, it was usually fair, but I did everything I could possibly do to avoid spankings and as a result became too good. I can remember days sitting in a chair with my hands folded in my lap, looking at a wall. I was far away inside, of course, but I would sit there and look 'good.' She didn't understand that that wasn't 'being good,' but it was important to her, so I did it.

"The sexual contact with this stepfather went on intermittently through my first year of high school, and I remember sitting on the edge of the bathtub thinking, 'A couple more years and I'll be sixteen, and they won't be able to make me do things.' By that time I was just living for the day I would be sixteen and could go out on my own. I used to say over and over to myself, 'I don't give a damn what anyone does to me, just let me get through high school. Survive. Survive.' Day after day, I existed for some unknown time in the future.

"During that time, my stepfather would go out and get drunk and come home and do things to me. I knew I had to stay a virgin; the church had taught me that. The only value I could keep for myself was to be a virgin, so I would let him do whatever he wanted as long as I stayed a virgin. While he was doing things, most of the time I wasn't even there. I was someplace else. My body was there but I wasn't.

"During high school, the house was in a constant state of upheaval. My resident stepfather left, an earlier one reappeared and there was no continuity to my life at all.

history of a survivor

I clung to the church because it was the one stable element in my life. I was at that time a very religious person, but the church was kind of a two-edged sword. I clung to it tighter and tighter because it was the only solid thing in my life, and as I clung to it the thorns kept going deeper and deeper into my own flesh. The pain was there, but the security was there, too. And my need was so great.

"I want to tell you about my mother, because it's important that people see that just because she wasn't a good mother doesn't mean there weren't reasons. Good reasons.

"The hardest part is trying to go back and figure out my relationship with my mother. It was mostly like I was her mother. In fact, I raised my mother from the time I can remember. I protected my mother. I can remember when I was eight or nine years old, and she'd come home from the tavern where she used to go and tell me about all her troubles and her trials. And she'd cry on my shoulder and I'd say, 'It's okay, Mom. You'll see. Things will get better. You'll see.' She just had so many problems to deal with.

"Most of the time her only social outlet was the bar. She was the first of her family to live in the city, and most of the people at the bar were strange to the city, too. The bar was a place where they could get together and talk about how things are going to be better tomorrow and about things that happened a long time ago on the farm. Most of those people were kind of frightened by the city, its bigness and its coldness, and they needed to huddle together in the bars to feel like they belonged someplace. Those were the only kind of men my mother ever met. We never went to movies or plays, and so all she met were those kind of men.

"She always worked. She was never without a job. She worked hard for us kids, keeping us in shoes and clothes and things. Most of the time she married for security, because they had jobs and she needed help with the kids, which she never really got.

181

conspiracy of silence

"I didn't see her often when I was a kid, and I guess when I was small I had her up on a pedestal, because in my mind she could do no wrong. If my mother did it, it had to be right. I don't really remember any talks at night, any intimacies, and she'd usually be drunk. She'd come home from the bar and expound on all of her troubles, cry on my shoulder and tell me how nasty and terrible men were, but how we needed them to help us.

"I used to try to please her so often and always seemed to fail. I wanted to please her, but no matter what I did it was never right, never good enough. Something was always wrong.

"In our neighborhood there were a lot of junk stores, and in one I saw an artificial corsage which was, I thought, the most beautiful thing I had ever seen in my life. I saved my lunch money for a week to buy it for my mother. When I brought it home to give to her, she looked at it and said, 'Gee, it's nice, but I wouldn't wear it to a dogfight.' That was so crushing, it's still hard to think about.

"When I was smaller and alone a lot, I used to pretend a world of my own in which I was the only real human being. I played with my dolls way up into high school, and it was *my* world. It was beautiful and complete, and it was clean. And most of all it was safe. No one could get to me when I was in my world.

"Sometimes I would see my mother and whatever stepfather copulating, and I would literally crawl out of bed, go outside and sit on the steps. It would be cold sometimes, but it was such a little house when I was small that I'd have to leave it to not see them. I'd sit on the steps and pray, 'Let me get through today. Let it be over when I get back in there.' They were drunk and slobbering. Something that should have been a very beautiful experience for a young woman to dream of, became for me a nightmare. It was something to be terrified of, something to run from. It got to the point that I could not see a naked man without getting physically nauseated.

history of a survivor

"You know, my mother had instincts like a mother cat. She always used to tell everybody, 'My kids are *my* kids. You don't take my kids, and you don't mess with my kids. That's the way it is.' She had an opportunity to marry a man who wanted to send my sister and me to a boarding school or day-care center, and she said no. I have to give her that. She tried, you know. She's really had a rough life, too. She could have left us many times, but she didn't, and somehow she managed to get through.

"In fact, my oldest sister, Ruth, had incest with my, our, father when she was nine. It had gone on for a while before she told. Mom had him arrested right away, and Ruth had to give testimony all by herself in closed court and sent him to jail for six months. Ruth never talked about it and neither did my mother. I don't remember any of it, I was still too little, but Ruth told me once. And we never talked about it anymore. She just tried to forget it. Like my mother tried to forget things. It was easier for her just to forget things because then she didn't have to feel guilty. My mother dealt with things by not dealing with them. Like putting them in a box, she called it, and putting them on a shelf. Now she says she can't pull the stuff out any-more—'It's too far back, it's too buried, I can't pull it out. I boxed it, labeled it and forgot it. That's that.'

"I was lucky in having other people to talk to all those years. Not about the sexual part of my life, but about all the rest. I used to spend a lot of time with neighbor ladies, and they were a real source of strength to me. They taught me that people could only do to you what you let them do. Of course, that made me feel guilty about what I had let them do, but I didn't say that. They'd remind me that there would be an end to what was going on, and I had to keep my dignity and keep as much of myself private as I could until such time as I could live on my own. I would tell them about the fighting and arguing at home, the end-less fights about drinking and money, the jealousy my stepfathers always had about my mother even though she never did anything to cause them to feel like that.

"While I was in grade school, I guess I was an emotionally disturbed child. But I was in Catholic school, and unless you were grossly disturbed it was kind of passed over as 'It's a passing phase and God will take care of it.' Well, God doesn't. And people don't take care of it either.

"Later on, in high school, I found a good priest, and we talked about a lot of things. And I found myself changing and thinking maybe I would be a nun when I finished college. This helped me keep my head together. It was a kind of goal for me.

"By the time I finally got out of high school and went away from home to college, I was sure I wanted to become a nun. But none of the convents would take me because of my emotional background. They'd ask you what kind of a home life you had had, and I'd tell them, trying to be up-front and honest. I'd lay it all out on the table—capsulized version, of course. But when I'd tell them, they would say they were sorry and that I wasn't material for the convent because I'd experienced too much. They would tell me the convent wasn't a place anybody could run to and hide in. It wasn't a secure haven to escape the bad things in the world.

"Now I can see that, but at the time it was very difficult for me. I have moved away from the church now because I can no longer be bothered with it. I can no longer feel close to a church that has no room for me. Why would I go through all of that, to find they have no room. They don't want me, so I'm not Catholic anymore.

"When I got away from home and began thinking about my mother, I became very angry and embittered with her. I never understood how she could live with me year after year and not see the despair and anger and frustration. How dare she call herself a mother? How could any person who had dragged me through what she had dragged me through call herself a mother? How dare she?

history of a survivor

"You see, I went to the other extreme, from total acceptance to total rejection of my mother. Finally, I began to
be able to think about good things she did, too. After all,
she had done the best she could as best she knew. She's a
perpetual teenager. Her family was very straightlaced and
uptight, and the primary thing in my grandparents' house
was discipline. There were a lot of kids, and it was mostly
grim, grinding poverty. They never talked about anything.
The summer my mother was eighteen, she fell in love and
got pregnant. She left home and didn't keep any contact
with any of them. That baby was my sister Ruth, and the
man was my father. Mother became the black sheep of her
family. She had wanted desperately to escape her family
and fall in love and laugh and have babies. But when she
got pregnant, she stopped growing. That one summer of
fun was all she had, and it turned out so bad it must have
scarred her. She never learned and kept getting caught in
the same circle over and over again, like a damaged phono-
graph record. I know she needs psychiatric help. She
needed help then and she still does, but it's not something
I could do for her. She's proud and won't accept help from
anybody, and she won't tell her private feelings to a stranger. That's just how she is. She decided long ago to keep
on going, and that's what she tries to do.

"When I ask my mother now if she's happy, she says,
'No, satisfied.' Even if I thought she had known or sensed
anything was going on when I was growing up, I would
suppress it. After all, when it's your mother, it's the only
mother you have. She was the only good thing in my
growing-up life, so she couldn't be bad, could she?

"I was very much afraid of men for years. I guess that's
normal for somebody who had a childhood like I did. But
I met a man four years ago, and he became my friend and
husband. He is a teacher, and I was so impressed when I
met him. He is kind and good, and nothing shocks him.
There is nothing so bad or so terrible that we can't talk

about it together. He comes from a large, boisterous Italian family with lots of cousins and laughing and fun. Of course, he had his problems, too, growing up. But his family is all on good terms, and I'm really glad because my son can have the joy of a large, loving family. It's such fun to be part of a family. I never really had anybody, and the loneliness of that has been a lot to bear.

"I think what allowed me to finally begin relating to men in a positive way is that, even when I was small, I always thought my stepfathers were exceptions rather than rules. I always kept a sense that there were other men out there who lived different lives. There were kids who had real fathers who were kind and normal. So I never really got so soured on men that I hated all of them. Now I'm married, and our sexual relationship finally is shaping up. For a long time I couldn't have a climax, but we have finally reached the point where I can. Sex has become a tender, loving, giving experience. I've developed enough trust with him so our sex gets better all the time.

"My mother lives with us now, and it's not always easy. She's sixty-five now, and she came to live with me because she was terribly lonely. After all those years of running around and all those men friends, she felt betrayed and used. She doesn't even go out anymore. She sits at the kitchen table and plays solitaire. But, you know, it's funny; she shows her guilt in very funny ways. She'll say for no reason at all, 'Well, it wasn't my fault that you got raised the way you did. I only did what I had to do.' Or she'll say, 'I'm sorry things were bad when you were growing up, but I didn't have any choice. Times were tough then. You had to survive. You had to toughen up. That's all you could do.'

"I sense that she knew and feels guilty. That she knew something, even if it wasn't specific. And as long as I never talked about it, it was best left unsaid and forgotten as fast as possible. Because what was she going to do?

history of a survivor

"I'm trying to work out my feelings about how to relate to her, adult to adult. She really shoulders the burden of cooking and cleaning in the house, since both my husband and I work. She actually is a great help, and she needs to feel she is living a useful life. She has to stay involved all the time. Right now her involvement is with her grandson and keeping her daughter's house.

"Slowly but surely I'm losing my need for blind beliefs—in the church and in my mother. That blindness and absolute dedication got me through and probably kept my sanity, but I don't want to give my child similar baggage to carry through his life. I didn't have any examples of healthy childhood, and I'm trying to read a lot and figure out how to do it right for my child. I need to remember my son is an individual who needs love and guidance and discipline, not punishment. I was so afraid of the world and of everything around me, I had no self-confidence. I don't want any child to have to work through such fear to keep their emotional balance. I do lots of things with my son that I wish I could have done as a child. We go to the park, the aquarium, the museum. I enjoy them as much as I enjoy watching him opening to new experiences. He is my link from the past, through now and into a real future. It is such a joy to see him grow and open.

"Recently I've begun telling my mother some of what I've mentioned here. I'm beginning to bring some of it out. I don't go into all the wretched details, but I want to share some of what I experienced, and I think she needs to know why I am the way I am.

"I often wonder why I survived and so many others don't. The scenes of my childhood are going on right now in thousands of homes all over the country. Those hidden children are me, and are like me, and I wish so desperately I could somehow reach them. Touch them gently. Tell them they're not alone."

LETTERS:
TO WHOM
IT MAY
CONCERN
♦♦♦♦♦♦♦

Letter to a young victim:

I suppose that if you have read this far, you have found
that at least parts of this book express some of the feelings
and experiences you have had. Your experiences have been
difficult, confusing and perhaps painful for you, and although I cannot lessen the hurting, I hope that knowing
you are not alone with your secret eases some of your pain.
These pages have been written about you, but they also
have been written for you, to help you feel the beginnings
of strength and seek alternatives to the silence—yours and
everybody else's. I held a picture of you in my mind as I
read and traveled and talked with people and wrote. It is
your face that has been before me, and it is to you that I
wish to speak first.

The most important thing I want to say to you is, "Please
tell someone about what is happening in your house." You
do not have to carry the heavy burden and responsibility
for what anyone else has done. Your secret will stop being
so painful once it has been revealed. When you share your

secret with someone, you join hands with another person and have the strength of two. And that is a start.

You are the only person who can decide who is the right person for you to reach out to. Think about all the people in your life and decide who is the most respectful, the most open and the most able to help you. It may seem hard to tell your mother, but sometimes she can be your best friend. Perhaps she won't believe you at first, because what you have to tell her is a difficult thing for mothers to believe. She may say that you're making it up or she may even get angry at you. But she may be willing to try to understand and help. If your mother is not the best person to tell, perhaps you can confide in a teacher, an aunt or the mother of one of your girlfriends. If not, there may be a women's organization in your town; you can call and ask to talk with someone there. If there is a college nearby, it may have a counseling program in which you can receive help and support. Or perhaps you know a priest, minister or rabbi who will listen and help.

The second important thing I want to tell you is that you are *not* responsible. Nobody, not even your parents, has the right to do anything to your mind or body that makes you feel bad or uncomfortable. And you are right to want to put an end to it. It is your body, and you can say no without feeling guilty.

I know there are times when you cannot say no to the person who is making you feel bad because grownups don't always listen to kids. But they do listen to other grownups, so that if you tell someone else, he or she can say no for you.

I understand that it's scary to think about telling your secret, but even though it's scary, it's much more lonesome to be silent and to keep all your feelings inside you. When you hear yourself telling someone about what is happening, you have begun to make it stop. It is the first and most important step toward defining your life and how you want to live it.

189

Letter to a child victim now grown:

I found myself thinking of you as I wrote to a child, our younger sister. Would it have made a difference, I wonder, if someone had written such a letter to you while you were still a child? Would your life have taken a different direction? I hope the future will be different for the young women who are reading this book, but for you, now grown, the painful experiences of childhood are woven into the fabric of your life.

As an adult woman, though, you have more control over your choices and can begin to make the necessary changes to break the bonds that tie you to a painful and unresolved past. For you, as for the child you once were, the primary need is to stop keeping your childhood experiences secret. Once you have acknowledged your past out loud, you can begin to find the help that you need. In seeking counsel and guidance for your life, you can begin to move forward personally. Furthermore, by talking about your past you can provide much needed support to other victims who still think they are alone. You can become someone to whom they can talk and unburden their feelings, someone who will hear and truly understand them.

You are the best resource not only for victims, but also for professionals in their efforts to develop the kinds of intervention and services that will be helpful to others still trapped in their family situations. In order for the medical and psychiatric communities to begin to imagine what your experiences have been like and how they can help you and other victims, you must talk with them—for you are the only one who really knows. You know how younger victims feel and can provide invaluable help in training professionals who are unskilled and uncertain in approaching the problem.

letters: to whom it may concern

In taking steps toward resolving your past and the pasts of countless others, you will be creating a circle within which the love, support and encouragement you offer will be returned a hundredfold. In speaking out, you will be providing a voice for other women who cannot yet speak for themselves. In becoming strong and insistent that all necessary measures be taken to provide communitywide programs for family intervention, your own life will become an example to children who have no one to show them how to grow into strong and powerful adult women.

Letter to a mother, a sister:

I know your position is a painful and difficult one, for in many ways you are caught in the middle. You may be blaming yourself or your child for what has happened in your family. You may be feeling conflicting loyalties toward your husband and your child. You may be feeling overwhelmed trying to decide whom to protect and whom to defend. This may be the most wrenching choice you have ever made, but I hope one of the clearest. Your husband does not need your protection and defense, for he is an adult who is responsible for his behavior. Your daughter is still a child and is vulnerable and powerless without your strength and support. She needs you to comfort her and help her to heal and to trust again.

But what about your needs? You may have learned well the lessons all of us women learn in subordinating our needs to the needs of others—sometimes our parents, at other times our children, but most often our husbands and other important men in our lives. We do the best we can to provide what others want from us, but all too often we sacrifice part of ourselves in the process. We learn to bury our feelings and pretend not to see what is before us because it is too painful or threatening, and we deny what is real in our lives for the sake of imagining what might be—if only *we* just try a little harder.

As women living in a male-dominated society, we have learned the same lessons. These lessons were taught to us everywhere we turned—in magazines, movies and school books—and they taught us to become the women we are. We have been taught, and we have believed, that it is "natural" to be the psychological, emotional and sexual service stations for the men in our lives. We have learned that we are only as important as our husbands are, and we value other women by their husbands in the same way.

It's a trap and it's a lie, and it has caused thousands of women like you and me a great loss. We have given our loyalty to people who have betrayed it, placed our trust in those who have abused it and hoped to derive our strength and sense of ourselves from others who could not provide them for us. However, all across our country we are beginning to detect the stirrings of anger—an anger that is beginning to change our lives. A community of women is growing, a community in which women find their strength inside themselves with the help of other women who are struggling to do the same thing. Women's groups are becoming forceful and assertive and are eager to provide you with the support and encouragement you may need to take that first step toward your child. For in protecting and defending her, in acknowledging that she is part of you, you will begin to move toward power and commitment in your life as a woman and mother and will become a model for future mothers.

Nearly all of the women with whom I spoke while I was writing this book told me that the most positive experience they had had in seeking to change their lives was in meeting with other women who had gone through similar experiences. There is something immeasurably comforting about sharing your feelings with a group of women who know and have felt what you are feeling now.

You don't have to deal with your family problem alone. It's not hard to find the women's groups and organizations that can help. Look in the white pages of your local phone book for listings that begin with the word "Women"; then call the one that seems most appropriate and begin to speak. Trust your sisters and in return they can help you to trust yourself.

Letter to a father, a brother:

It is not what you have felt about your child that is damaging; many parents have thought and felt many of the same things. It is what you have done about those feelings that has been so harmful to your child, your family and you. I cannot pretend to be non-judgmental because I strongly believe that a judgment must be made, responsibility acknowledged and restitution made.

When you read the stories of fathers who behaved in ways that you have, could you hear yourself speaking? Again and again they insisted that it was everybody's fault but their own, insisted that they couldn't help themselves. However, it does not matter what your child may have worn, however skimpy or attractive, and it does not matter what she may have said or done; for you are an adult, and with you alone rests the accountability for placing control and limits on your behavior. If you cannot remain in your home without continuing to damage the children within it, then you must take it upon yourself to leave. It is with you that the cycle can and must be broken.

I am judging your behavior, not your humanity. No matter what you have done in the past, you have the potential for change. But in order to change, you first must make the commitment to try. There comes a point when blame, recrimination and past anger and resentment are no longer reasons to cling to old ways of living. What happened to you when you were a child and what your relationships with your wife and friends may have been like do not matter; what does matter is that you find a way to go forward from what went before.

You *can* help yourself, you *can* stop what you have been doing and you *can* begin to change. Not to prove yourself to anyone, not to try to erase what you already have done, but so you can look in the mirror when you are alone and feel a sense of pride in having reconstructed your life. I hope you want to do that for yourself, to make sense out of your past and to begin to develop some hope for your future. It is up to you, and nobody else, to take the reins of your life and to make your life what you want it to be.

There are people who will help, but first you must ask for help and understand that the work will be hard and painful. Whether it is your priest or a therapist or an old army buddy, begin wherever you can. That beginning will become the first step away from your past and toward a different future.

Letter to families and friends:

I imagine that parts of this book were uncomfortable reading for you. Perhaps the experiences related here brought up feelings you had for someone in your family or things that happened to you or around you when you were a child. By denying that these things happened or that they upset you in any way, you may have kept yourself from recognizing that such feelings and experiences are common, that they are not unique to your life.

But acknowledging your own feelings and experiences is just the first step. There are others in your family who still harbor such secrets—things they have never said aloud and feelings they will not permit themselves to think about. Once you have taken that first, honest look at your own life and feelings, you can encourage others to do the same. It is quite extraordinary how less burdensome our innermost feelings become once we have shared them with others who care about us.

How you respond to a family in which incestuous assault occurs is directly related to how you respond to your own hidden feelings and to the silence of your family. Light is needed in all the dark places, and fresh air must be introduced into the musty silences and buried nightmares.

You can begin by listening to the members of your own family, and from there you can reach out to other troubled families you may know. You don't have to do much to help. The hardest part is being able to move beyond the shock and aversion which stigmatize the incest family, isolate the child victim and allow the abuse to continue. Working to lower your anxiety and discomfort with the idea of incest can help you become an ally to those who need your friendship and support. All you may need to do is make a pot of coffee, sit at your kitchen table and listen. Your openness to hearing those first halting words makes a tremendous difference. Your outstretched hand has the potential to change many lives, including your own.

If each of us truly listens, we can learn much from each other; then we can begin to move beyond our judgments, preconceptions and separateness and begin to heal.

Letter to professionals:

Much of this book may have seemed unduly harsh and biased to you. It is. For as I traveled and heard you say that you have dealt with few incestuous assault cases in your programs, agencies and departments, I saw the same wall of backs seen by families who desperately need your help and services. There are no simple answers to the questions and problems that have been raised in this book. The best any of us can do is to make a first step, a beginning that will challenge society's denial of the problem and help us to meet our obligation to provide services and alternatives for incestuous assault victims. Some communities are beginning to find the courage to examine the reality of incestuous abuse. Not often, not enough, but at least—at last—a beginning.

How can we as psychological and physiological healers help to foster realistic, healthy sex roles? How can we go about changing society's ignorance about basic human sexuality? How can we share the responsibility for human problems outside the realm of our own experiences and reach out to children whose unhealed wounds and undefended spirits are an emotionally cancerous legacy passed from generation to generation?

These problems are difficult ones, and the solutions are not simple or clear. But without all existing community resources working together to provide help to incest families, the problems will continue and grow.

I have some suggestions. They may need to be altered to meet the specific needs of individual communities across the country, but I offer them as guidelines and as a place to begin.

I know most of us spend many hours in meetings—meetings in which little is accomplished, in which professional "turf" is protected and in which personal egos often get in the way of creating necessary changes within each of our own "families." I am suggesting still other kinds of meetings, in which all agencies and organizations within a discipline that are interested or skilled in any aspect of the problems associated with incestuous assault get together to define priorities and set up procedures for the protection of abused children and others within incest families. Emphasis will vary from agency to agency, but by clarifying our philosophies and approaches we can develop a more effective communitywide team approach to the problem.

In every community, child-protection service agencies first and foremost must serve as children's advocates and bring whatever pressure is needed upon other helping agencies to respond to the needs of victims and their families. Emphasis on recruitment and training of larger staffs is a way to broaden the services these agencies might provide. The priority of such agencies is clear and simple: to protect children in the best way possible.

The medical community does not have so clear a mandate. Physicians and nurses are not trained as catalysts of social change and are taught to heal visible body wounds, not unseen emotional scars and bruises. The participation of medical personnel most likely to come into contact with young victims and their families—hospital emergency-room personnel as well as pediatrics, family services and obstetrics/gynecology specialists—in meetings with child-protection service workers will result in a pooling of knowledge about case presentation, suspicious symptoms, identification, reporting obligations and appropriate referral sources.

Those who are involved in some part of the criminal justice system can meet with police, parole officers, defense and prosecuting attorneys and judges to discuss ways to develop consistent legal protocol that can make laws work *for* the members of incest families rather than *against* them.

Psychiatrists, psychologists, family counselors and therapists along with other mental health professionals can meet to share their knowledge and experience concerning the psychodynamics of the incest family. Sharing this information will raise the general level of expertise and sensitivity in counseling by making such knowledge more widely accessible to counselors with clients who are trying to come to terms with incest experiences.

Those who work in our schools as teachers, curriculum planners, guidance counselors and administrators can meet to begin developing programs to teach children clearer truths about their sexuality and to acquaint educators with behavior patterns common to young incest victims. This can be done in partnership with local health departments, which may be able to develop materials and programs for in-service training to be supplied by public health nurses.

Social service agencies, youth guidance facilities, foster-care services, religious leaders, women's and men's organizations—everyone who is in a position to help or is concerned enough to become involved—can meet to provide input and encourage professional groups to develop programs to aid incest families.

Once preliminary interagency meetings within each profession have been held, then representatives from each discipline can meet together. In some communities, this may be the first time professionals have been exposed to the pressures surrounding each other's concerns and priorities. Because incestuous assault is a multi-dimensional problem requiring the joint effort of all community groups, all strata of society are needed to provide insight for developing comprehensive programs of education, identification, wholistic treatment and prevention.

I strongly recommend that you include one particular group of people in all your discussions: incest victims. In our communities, neighborhoods, families, churches and schools, children must be encouraged to tell us in their own words whatever they are experiencing that is troublesome for them. We must make ourselves available to listen to young people, because unless we give them the opportunity to talk about their experiences so that we can learn from them, we cannot develop sensitive, effective programs. Incest victims are the best resource we have in developing effective means to deal with their problems. We must find constructive ways to respond to their needs.

In all of our meetings, we need to express strong opinions about how to intervene successfully in incestuous assault situations, for children must have the absolute right to safety, dignity and freedom from any form of abuse, whether it be physical, emotional or sexual. Although each community must develop its own agenda for the possibly heated and difficult discussions that will take place at these meetings, the following issues provide a place to begin:

· Where can a child victim of incestuous assault go for medical examination, counseling and emotional support if the child does not want his or her parents to know about the request for help? What is the helping agency allowed to do for the young person and what is it required to do in such a case?

· If a parent or adult relative is willing to report an incestuous assault, to whom does he or she report? What will happen after the report is made? What existing follow-up procedures will go into effect?

· If a parent or other close adult strongly suspects that incestuous abuse is occurring and is not willing to report it to an agency, what can he or she do? What resources does your community have for providing intervention?

· If a non-involved adult—a teacher, hotline counselor, neighbor or friend—believes that there is incestuous abuse within a family, what can this person do? To whom does he or she report? What will happen?

· If incestuous assault has been identified and confirmed, how can the child's statements be taken in a non-threatening manner? How can the truth of such alternative methods of testimony be assured in a court of law? How can the child best be protected from intimidation and pressure throughout legal proceedings?

· If the incestuous assault is determined to be ongoing, what is done with and for the child? What is done for other siblings in the home? What treatment is offered to the aggressor and the child's mother?

· How can the professionals in your community expand their skills and capacity to deal with incestuous assault cases?

· What agency in your community has primary responsibility for providing intervention for child victims and what monitoring procedures are being used to determine the effectiveness of its work?

Interagency and interdisciplinary meetings initiated in cities and towns throughout the country can be the beginning of breaking the historic, intergenerational patterns of incestuous assault, to move us beyond ourselves to the thousands of grown-up children who have learned that isolation, estrangement, guilt, powerlessness and rage are their bitter portion of the American Dream. We can . . . and we must.

Appendix A

California State Penal Code Sections
Relating to Child Sexual Abuse

Penal Code Section	Subject Matter	Maximum Penalty for First Offense
220	Assault with intent to commit rape, sodomy, etc.	Felony: two, three or four years in state prison
261	Rape (females over the age of eighteen)	Felony: three, four or five years in state prison
261.5	Unlawful sexual intercourse (with a female under the age of eighteen)	Felony: sixteen months, or two or three years in state prison
272	Contributing to the delinquency of a minor (person under the age of eighteen)	Misdemeanor: up to one year in county jail or fine not exceeding $2,500, or both; or probation not exceeding five years
273(a)(1)	Infliction of physical or mental suffering on a child or endangering his or her health under circumstances likely to result in great bodily injury or death	Felony: sixteen months, or two or three years in state prison
273(a)(2)	Same as (1), but occurs under circumstances in which the child's life is not in immediate danger	Misdemeanor: up to six months in county jail or fine not exceeding $500, or both
273(d)	Infliction of unusual or inhuman punishment on a child resulting in traumatic injury	Felony: sixteen months, or two or three years in state prison
273(g)	Immoral practices in the presence of a child	Misdemeanor: up to six months in county jail or fine not exceeding $500, or both
285	Incest	Felony: sixteen months, or two or three years in state prison

appendix

Penal Code Section	Subject Matter	Maximum Penalty for First Offense
286	Sodomy	
	Victim under eighteen	Felony: sixteen months, or two or three years in state prison
	Offender is over twenty-one, victim under sixteen	Felony: sixteen months, or two or three years in state prison
	Offender is more than ten years older than victim, who is under fourteen; or by force or violence	Felony: two, three or four years in state prison
	Acting in concert with force	Felony: three, four or five years in state prison
288	Child-molesting: lewd and lascivious conduct with a child under fourteen with intent to gratify lusts of victim or accused	Felony: three, four or five years in state prison
288(a)	Oral copulation	
	Victim under eighteen	Felony: sixteen months, or two or three years in state prison
	Offender is over twenty-one, victim under sixteen	Felony: sixteen months, or two or three years in state prison
	Offender is more than ten years older than victim, who is under fourteen; or by force or violence	Felony: two, three or four years in state prison
	Acting in concert with force	Felony: three, four or five years in state prison
647(a)	Child-molesting: annoy and molest a child under eighteen	Misdemeanor: up to six months in county jail or fine not exceeding $500, or both

Compiled from *Deering's Penal Code, Annotated, of the State of California,* Sections 1-718 (San Francisco: Bancroft-Whitney, 1971), and *Deering's Penal Code, Annotated, of the State of California, 1977 Pocket Supplement,* Sections 1-718.

Appendix B

Mandatory Child-Abuse Reporting
Law for California

§11166. [Duty of observer] (a) Except as provided in subdivision (b), any child care custodian, medical practitioner, nonmedical practitioner, or employee of a child protective agency who has knowledge of or observes a child in his or her professional capacity or within the scope of his or her employment whom he or she knows or reasonably suspects has been the victim of child abuse shall report the known or suspected instance of child abuse to a child protective agency immediately or as soon as practically possible by telephone and shall prepare and send a written report thereof within 36 hours of receiving the information concerning the incident. For the purposes of this article, "reasonable suspicion" means that it is objectively reasonable for a person to entertain such a suspicion, based upon facts that could cause a reasonable person in a like position, drawing when appropriate on his or her training and experience, to suspect child abuse.

(b) Any child care custodian, medical practitioner, nonmedical practitioner, or employee of a child protective agency who has knowledge of or who reasonably suspects that mental suffering has been inflcited on a child or his or her emotional well-being is endangered in any other way, may report such known or suspected instance of child abuse to a child protective agency.

(c) Any commercial film and photographic print processor who has knowledge of or observes, within the scope of his or her professional capacity or employment, any film, photograph, video tape, negative or slide depicting a child under the age of 14 years engaged in an act of sexual conduct, shall report such instance of suspected child abuse to the law enforcement agency having jurisdiction over the case immediately or as soon as practically possible by telephone and shall prepare and send a written report of it with a copy of the film, photograph, video tape, negative or slide attached within 36 hours of receiving the information concerning the incident. As used in this subdivision, "sexual conduct" means any of the following:

(1) Sexual intercourse, including genital-genital, oral-genital, anal-genital, or oral-anal, whether between persons of the same or opposite sex or between humans and animals.

(2) Penetration of the vagina or rectum by any object.

(3) Masturbation, for the purpose of sexual stimulation of the viewer.

(4) Sadomasochistic abuse for the purpose of sexual stimulation of the viewer.

(5) Exhibition of the genitals, pubic or rectal areas of any person for the purpose of sexual stimulation of the viewer.

(d) Any other person who has knowledge of or observes a child whom he or she knows or reasonably suspects has been a victim of child abuse may report the known or suspected instance of child abuse to a child protective agency.

(e) When two or more persons who are required to report are present and jointly have knowledge of a known or suspected instance of child abuse, and when there is agreement among them, the telephone report may be made and signed by such selected member of the reporting team. Any member who has knowledge that the member designated to report has failed to do so, shall thereafter make the report.

(f) The reporting duties under this section are individual, and no supervisor or administrator may impede or inhibit the reporting duties and no person making such a report shall be subject to any sanction for making the report. However, internal procedures to facilitate reporting and apprise supervisors and administrators of reports may be established provided that they are not inconsistent with the provisions of this article.

(g) A county probation or welfare department shall immediately or as soon as practically possible report by telephone to the law enforcement agency having jurisdiction over the case, to the agency given the responsibility for investigation of cases under Section 300 of the Welfare and Institutions Code, and to the district attorney's office every known or suspected instance of child abuse as defined in Section 11165, except acts or omissions coming within the provisions of paragraph (2) of subdivision (c) of Section 11165, which shall only be reported to the county welfare department. A county probation or welfare department shall also send a written report thereof within 36 hours of receiving the information concerning the incident to any agency to which it is required to make a telephone report under this subdivision.

A law enforcement agency shall immediately or as soon as practically possible report by telephone to the county welfare department, the agency given responsibility for investigation of cases under Section 300 of the Welfare and Institutions Code, and to the district attorney's office every known or suspected instance of child abuse reported to it, except acts or omissions coming within the provisions of paragraph (2) of subdivision (c) of Section 11165, which shall only be reported to the county welfare department. A law enforcement agency shall also send a written report thereof within 36 hours of receiving the information concerning the incident to any agency to which it is required to make a telephone report under this subdivision. Amended Stats 1984 ch 1423 §9, effective September 26, 1984.

NOTES

The Scope of the Problem

1. Vincent DeFrancis, ed., *Sexual Abuse of Children* (Denver: American Humane Association, Children's Division, 1969), pp. 56 and 66.
2. Herbert Maisch, *Incest*, p. 69.
3. DeFrancis, *Protecting the Child Victim of Sex Crimes Committed by Adults*, p. vii.
4. *Ibid.*
5. *Sacramento Union*, February 6, 1977.
6. Suzanne Sgroi, "Sexual Molestation of Children. The Last Frontier in Child Abuse," p. 20.
7. S. Kirson Weinberg, *Incest Behavior*, p. 39.
8. *On the Road: The Runaway Newsletter* (Los Angeles: Institute of Scientific Analysis), Summer 1975, p. 1, as cited in *Child Sexual Abuse* (San Jose, Calif.: NOW Child Sexual Abuse Task Force, 1976).
9. Ellen Weber, "Incest: Sexual Abuse Begins at Home," p. 65.
10. Ann Burgess and Lynda Holmstrom, "Sexual Trauma of Children and Adolescents: Pressure, Sex and Secrecy," *Nursing Clinics of North America* 10: 552-53.
11. Jean Benward and Judianne Densen-Gerber, *Incest as a Causative Factor in Anti-Social Behavior: An Exploratory Study* (New York: Odyssey Institute, 1975), p. 6.
12. Judson T. Landis, "Experiences of 500 Children with Adult Sexual Deviation," *Psychiatric Quarterly Supplement* 30 (pt.1):93.
13. Joseph J. Peters, "Children Who Are Victims of Sexual Assault and the Psychology of Offenders," *American Journal of Psychotherapy* 30:415.

The Children

1. Lauretta Bender and Abram Blau, "The Reaction of Children to Sexual Relationships with Adults," *American Journal of Orthopsychiatry* 7 (1937):514.
2. As cited in Eileen Ogintz, "The Street's No Home Either," *National Observer*, November 20, 1976, p. 1.
3. Robin Lloyd, *For Money or Love: Boy Prostitution in America*, p. 212.

The Aggressors

1. Roland Summit and Joann Kryso, "Sexual Abuse of Children: A Clinical Spectrum," in press.
2. Judith Herman and Lisa Hirschman, "Father-Daughter Incest," p. 749.
3. Hector Cavallin, "Incestuous Fathers: A Clinical Report," p. 1134.

The Mothers

1. Irving Kaufman, Alice L. Peck and Consuelo K. Tagiuri, "The Family Constellation and Overt Incestuous Relations between Father and Daughter," *American Journal of Orthopsychiatry* 24 (1954):269-70.
2. Judith Herman and Lisa Hirschman, "Father-Daughter Incest," p. 746.
3. Yvonne Tormes, *Child Victims of Incest*, p. 35.

notes

The Family

1. Sol Gordon, "A Strong Case for Straightforward Sex Education in the Home and the School," *American School Board Journal,* February 1975, p. 39.

The Professional Family

1. Suzanne Sgroi, "Sexual Molestation of Children. The Last Frontier in Child Abuse," p. 19.
2. Ray Helfer, "The Reluctant Samaritans," *Emergency Medicine,* March 1975, p. 122.
3. *Ibid.*
4. Sgroi, p. 20.
5. Doris Stevens and Lucy Berliner, *Special Techniques for Child Witnesses* (Washington, D.C.: Center for Women's Policy Studies, 1976), p. 5.
6. Leroy Schultz, "Child Sex Victim: Social, Psychological and Legal Perspectives," p. 150.

RECOMMENDED BIBLIOGRAPHY

First Person/Anthologies/Self Help

Allen,Charlotte V. *Daddy's Girl.* New York: Wyndham, 1980.

Angelou, Maya. *I Know Why The Caged Bird Sings.*New York: Bantam Books, 1971.

Armstrong, Louise. *Kiss Daddy Goodnight.* New York: Hawthorn, 1978.

Bass, Ellen & Thornton, Louise. (Eds.) *I Never Told Anyone: Writings By Women Survivors of Child Sexual Assault.* New York: Harper & Row, 1983.

Brady, Katherine. *Father's Days.* New York: Dell, 1980.

Freespirit, Judy. *Daddy's Girl: An Incest Survivor's Story.* Langlois OR: Diaspora Press, 1982.

Gil, Eliana. *Outgrowing The Pain: A Book For And About Adults Abused As Children.* San Francisco: Launch Press, 1983.

Marie, Linda. *I Must Not Rock.* New York: Daughters Publishing, 1977.

McNaron, Toni A.H. & Morgan, Yarrow. *Voices In The Night.* Minneapolis MN: Cleis Press, 1982.

Morris, Michelle. *If I Should Die Before I Wake.* Los Angeles: J.P. Tarcher, 1982.

Feminist Analysis: Theory & Practice

Briere, John. "The Effects of Childhood Sexual Abuse on Later Psychological Functioning: Defining A Post-Sexual-Abuse Syndrome." Paper delivered to the Third National Conference on Sexual Victimization of Children at Childrens Hospital, National Medical Center, Washington DC, April, 1984.

"Child Sexual Assault." *Aegis* (Fall, 1980).(Box 21033, Washington DC 20009).

Conte, J.R. & Berliner, L. "Sexual Abuse of Children: Implications For Practice." *Social Casework* 63 (1981): 601-616.

Conte, J.R. & Shore, D., Eds. *Social Work And Child Sexual Abuse.* New York: Haworth, 1982.

Courtois, C. & Watts, D. "Counseling Adult Women Who Experienced Incest In Childhood or Adolescence." *Personnel & Guidance Journal* (1982): 275-279.

Finkelhor, David. *Child Sexual Abuse: New Theory & Research.* New York: Free Press, 1984.

Finkelhor, David. *Sexually Victimized Children.* New York: Free Press, 1979.

Fortune, Marie. *Sexual Violence: The Unmentionable Sin: An Ethical and Pastoral Perspective.* New York: Pilgrim, 1983.

Gager, N. & Schurr, C. *Sexual Assault: Confronting Rape in America.* San Francisco: Jossey-Bass, 1980.

Groth, A. Nicholas, Hobson, W. & Gary T. "The Child Molester: Clinical Observations" In J. Conte, & D. Shore, Eds. In *Social Work and Child Sexual Abuse.* New York: Haworth, 1982.

Herman, J.L., Schatzow, E. "Time-Limited Group Therapy for Women With a History of Incest." *International Journal of Group Psychotherapy* 34 (1984): 605-614.

Herman, J.L. *Father-Daughter Incest.* Cambridge: Harvard University Press, 1981.

Leonard, Linda S. *The Wounded Woman.* Boulder CO: Shambhala, 1982.

MacFarlane, K., Jones, B. & Jenstrom, L. *Sexual Abuse of Children: Selected Readings.* Washington:DHHS, 1980.

Miller, Alice. *For Your Own Good.* New York: Farrar, Straus, & Giroux, 1983.

Miller, Alice. *Thou Shalt Not Be Aware.* New York: Farrar, Straus, & Giroux, 1984.

Rush, Florence. *The Best Kept Secret: Sexual Abuse of Children.* New York: Prentice Hall, 1980.

Russell, Diana E.H. *Sexual Exploitation: Rape, Child Sexual Abuse and Sexual Harassment.* Beverly Hills: Sage, 1984.

Russell, Diana E.H. *The Secret Trauma: Incest in the Lives of Girls and Women.* New York: Basic Books, 1986 (in press).

Sgroi, Suzanne M. *Handbook of Clinical Intervention in Child Sexual Assault.* Lexington MA: D.C. Heath, 1982.

Summit, Roland. "Beyond Belief: The Reluctant Discovery of Incest." In M. Kirkpatrick, Ed., *Women In Context*. New York: Plenum, 1981.

Summit, Roland. "The Child Sexual Abuse Accommodation Syndrome." *Child Abuse and Neglect*. 7 (1983): 177-193.

Summit, Roland. "Recognition and Treatment of Child Sexual Abuse." In C. Hollingsworth, Ed., *Providing For The Emotional Health of the Pediatric Patient*. New York: Spectrum, 1981.

Ward, Elizabeth. *Father-Daughter Rape*. London: The Women's Press, 1984.

Children/Prevention/Programs

Adams, Caren, Fay, Jennifer and Loreen-Martin, Jan. *No Is Not Enough: Helping Teenagers Avoid Sexual Assault*. San Luis Obispo CA: Impact, 1984.

Adams, Caren, Fay, Jennifer. *No More Secrets: Protecting Your Child From Sexual Assault*. San Luis Obispo CA: Impact, 1981.

Chetin, Helen. *Frances Ann Speaks Out: My Father Raped Me*. Stanford: New Seed Press, 1977.

Child Assault Prevention Project. *Strategies For Free Children: A Leader's Guide To Child Assault Prevention*. Columbus OH: CAPP (P.O. Box 02084).

Colao, Flora & Hosansky, Tamar. *Your Child Should Know*. New York: Bobbs-Merrill, 1983.

Fay, Jennifer. *He Told Me Not To Tell*. Renton WA: King County Rape Relief, 1979.

Fay, Jennifer & Flerchinger, Billie Jo. *Top Secret: Sexual Assault Information For Teenagers Only*. Renton WA: King County Rape Relief, 1979.

Giaretto, Henry A. *Integrated Treatment of Child Sexual Abuse*. Palo Alto CA: Science & Behavior Books, 1982.

Knopp, Fay Honey. *Retraining Adult Sex Offenders: Methods & Models*. Syracuse NY: Safer Society, 1984.

Knopp, Fay Honey. *Remedial Intervention In Adolescent Sex Offenses: Nine Program Descriptions*. Syracuse NY: Safer Society, 1984.

Sanford, Linda T. *Come Tell Me Right Away: A Positive Approach*. Fayetteville NY: Ed-U Press, 1982.

Sanford, Linda T. *The Silent Children: A Book For Parents About The Prevention Of Child Sexual Abuse*. Garden City NY: McGraw-Hill, 1982.

Stowell, Jo & Dietzel, Mary. *My Very Own Book About Me*. Spokane WA: Lutheran Social Services of Washington, 1980.

Talking About Touching. Seattle WA: Committee for Children, Curriculums for Pre-school, Elementary and Junior High (P.O. Box 15190).

Wachter, Oralee. *No More Secrets For Me*. Boston: Little, Brown & Co., 1983.

THE PROBLEM RECONSIDERED

As I read the words I wrote eight years ago, I suspect that this is, in many ways, a kinder book than the one I would now write. Kinder and more patient. I was writing then and now directly to the woman who is beginning to remember and acknowledge her sexual assault and to be able to speak of it to others. During these intervening years, I have witnessed the breaking of silence on many occasions and still continue to marvel at the determination such a transformative act requires. For once the experience is given language—language to name it as an assault and to hold the perpetrator responsible—the first irrevocable steps toward healing have begun. I have been a partner to and observer of the efforts of women struggling against the amnesia that often served as defense against the feelings of pain, rage and loss which such assault generates in the life of a small child. But becoming survivors, victims have spoken out and ended their silence. The acts of courage displayed by survivors, even when the response has been disbelief, denial, blame or punishment, have taught me invaluable lessons about both the price and reward of survival.

As this issue has emerged into public consciousness, possibilities exist that were unimaginable eight years ago. Girls and women in greater numbers are shifting from privately adapting to an intolerable environment to establishing a community with others who have experienced histories similar to their own. And there are thousands of women who have triumphed over their abusive early lives with resiliency and tenacity. These words are primarily to celebrate them for engaging in their painful history and insisting that the professional and activist community join them in their healing work.

The sexual abuse of children by both members of the

family as well as older children and adults outside of it has become a discrete field of study with its own unique dimensions and emerging patterns. Ongoing work is being done to better understand the frequency of assault, who is victimized, new ways to recognize and intervene in the early stages of victimization, common responses of victimized children, long-term defensive adaptations, and the growing need for counseling services and legal recourse based on a child-advocacy model. This new field is a direct result of the perseverance of survivors and their feminist supporters, both professional and activist, as well as their insistence on information, resources, and organizations staffed with trained people who are dedicated to providing services that are supportive, safe and non-judgmental.

Much has been done, yet much remains. As we learn more about the sexual abuse of children, we are gaining a new recognition of the complexities of this problem. When *Conspiracy of Silence* was first published, most information focused on father or step-father assaults, systemic dynamics and family patterns. We now understand that offenders are a highly differentiated population: biological fathers and step-fathers, brothers, cousins, and grandfathers within the family, to authority figures, trusted friends and neighbors outside the family circle, to strangers and older children in the community at large. We are learning about the tricks, bribes and deception most commonly used to gain access and compliance from a child, in addition to force, threats and violence. Abused children are younger than we had previously imagined, and include a significant number of boys as well. Additionally, pornography is frequently used to gain access to the child and can be incorporated into the assault itself. We are discovering well-organized rings of adults who sexually abuse their own and other people's children.

The problem is bigger and more complex than we had thought and it has resulted in renewed efforts through research, clinical training, and community education to reach children and adults who are at risk.

Feminist analysis of the social factors implicit in the sexual abuse of women and children have repeatedly confirmed that sexual violence is predominantly the behavior of adolescent boys and adult men. There appears to be a "gender-gap" in sexual molestation. In other words, sexual abuse has a gender and it is male.

While there are some reports of female abusers, their numbers remain small and quite disproportionate within the alarming statistical range of abusers. Male offenders seem to come in all sizes, shapes, colors and ages. Some are chemically dependent or alcoholic; others are teetotalers or religious fundamentalists; some are chronically unemployed and yet others are successful and accomplished professional men; some have excellent social skills and others are isolated and rarely interact with others. While their individual behavior takes many forms, it is behavior that is primarily male.

There are several implications in thinking about sexual abuse as male behavior with the greater power afforded males in this society. The first is in the widely shared focus and priority in most counseling programs to re-unite families in which sexual abuse occurs. Mental health professionals and family therapists define the traditional nuclear family as the basic unit to be preserved at all costs. The family is viewed as a dysfunctional system (which it often is) with little ability to tolerate stress, change, conflict or the separate development and lives of each of its members. Further, for many reasons, the mother is sometimes unable to intervene successfully in the defense and protection of her child. While some of these dynamics may apply in some families, to reduce our analysis to intrapsychic and interpersonal formulations results in several dangerous consequences. It is woman-blaming, holding the mother responsible for the behavior of the male adult and expecting her to be the source of all emotional sustenance in the family. It offers the offender a range of excuses, defenses and rationalizations to avoid his sole responsibility, and finally, it does not take into account the inherent power imbalance in family life. The fundamental fact remains—families do not molest children —men do.

The increasing focus on reunifying the family after a sexual assault further traps the mother and her children into a closed system with a sexual offender. The helping agencies and the criminal justice system inadvertently collude to perpetuate a bad situation, since many women fear their own ability to provide for themselves emotionally, physically and financially. Taking the offender back into the family after minimal (if any) punishment, cursory treatment and some limited counseling, too often seems the only solution. We need instead, to develop the potential resources and skills of the mother and her children. By counseling them individually and together, we can offer re-unification as one of many choices, only after they have developed some real alternatives. Allowing an incestuous offender back into a family without sufficient punishment or treatment may not be an act of forgiveness or of love, but rather an act of desperation in the complete absence of other choices. Maintaining the family unit ought to be less important than the protection and strengthening of the women and children in that unit.

As long as we continue to condone a structure of family life based on a unit headed by a patriarchal figure, however benevolent, we may be implicitly endangering the lives of the women and children in that unit. Feminist theory reminds us that even as we deal with individual acts of sexual and physical violence committed by men, it is the power concentrated in the hands of one gender that is the fundamental social problem.

The second implication of this analysis results in a need to reassess the current emphasis given to the psychological precursors to a criminal act. Mental health professionals frequently focus on the nature of the male's early relationships, the ways he feels satisfied (or unsatisfied) in his present life situation, his skills or lack of them in managing stress and tension, his impulse control and substance abuse patterns and his relationships with his wife and mother. This focus provides the sex offender a safety net of psychological excuses and often outright denial either of the assault or of its seriousness to his victim.

Frequently, punishment is seen as overly "punitive" and the often preferred intervention is that of reconciliation, after an often cursory apology to family members. We worry about arresting and punishing offenders and re-define what is criminal behavior as "loving unwisely." When a man breaks into a store and steals from it, the response of the criminal justice system is clear and une-quivocal. When the offense however, is to break into the body of a small child and steal the childhood that child has a right to enjoy, we grow confused about the nature of the behavior, calling it psychological rather than criminal. The sexual abuse of children is a crime, first and foremost. Treatment can and should begin after that recognition and an appropriate legal response has been made.

The third implication is the need to redefine "genera-tional transmission." Many believe that children who were abused grow up to become abusers. While this certainly generates sympathy for abusers, it does not reflect the reality that the majority of children who are sexually abus-ed are girls. We are then left to wonder why there are not vastly higher numbers of female perpetrators. While both boys and girls are abused and both equally suffer the catastrophic loss of innocence and sense of safety in the world, they learn very different lessons. A girl who is sex-ually abused is more likely to grow up to become a victim of rape or wife-beating as an adult. She is also more likely to choose a partner who mirrors her own lowered sense of self-esteem and will be ineffective in either her own behalf or that of her children. While girls grow into women who remain trapped in the repetitive patterns of adaptions that the assault required, a significant number of abused boys grow into men who sexually abuse others.

A final consequence of this analysis is the growing awareness that to be a "good" child is to be a vulnerable child. Not questioning adult authority, distrusting their own ability and instincts to correctly assess potentially dangerous situations, an absence of strategizing skills and the right to say no and resist unwanted touching by older children or adults, all make a child vulnerable. Like molesters, children who are molested come in all sizes, shapes, colors, races and class backgrounds. To be a child however, is to have less power than those who molest. Equalizing that fundamental power imbalance is the field of child assault prevention work. Alternately called training in personal safety rights, crime-prevention or sexual assault prevention—these plays, pamphlets, books, films and train-ed prevention educators provide children information about molestation and the resources that are available to them in the event of possible assault.

While prevention efforts are doubling, so is a vocal and powerful backlash. Teaching children about sexual abuse, about self-defense, indeed, about sexuality, is being challenged by those who represent conservative and tradi-tional family structure. Day care, rather than being seen as an invaluable resource for working parents and their children, is being harshly labeled as a "breeding ground" for molesters. Professionals in the field of child sexual abuse know that generally just the opposite is true. Day care centers are filled with women and men who care about and are advocates for children. They are as eager as the general public to be sure their centers are safe and nur-turant environments for the children in their charge.

Further, it is being suggested that children "make-up" their stories of molestation and should not be trusted. However, we know that children go to great lengths to convince us that sexual abuse has *not* happened—not that it has. It is much more common for a child to protect the offending adult than to try to protect herself. But, while this backlash poses a challenge to the work that is being done, it is a challenge that can be met. Information is the best weapon that we have; information about sexuality, about molestation, about safe and strong behavior by children and adults.

For all these reasons, the book I would write today would be less kind, less patient. I would emphasize the relationship of power and gender to the issue of sexual abuse. I would examine family life in a more critical way and stress the crucial importance of providing children with the information they need to join us, as caring adults, in protecting themselves from abusive adults. I would urge us all to take our example from survivors and begin the sometimes dangerous business of speaking clearly about the silences that remain. It will not be a popular act and one that may carry the possibility of personal or professional repercussion. But we cannot allow our friends and clients, our sisters and daughters to stand alone. We too must speak, honor the words of survivors and add our own voices and visions to theirs.